Getting Started with Kudu
Perform Fast Analytics on Fast Data

*Jean-Marc Spaggiari, Mladen Kovacevic,
Brock Noland, and Ryan Bosshart*

Beijing · Boston · Farnham · Sebastopol · Tokyo

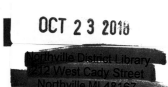

Getting Started with Kudu

by Jean-Marc Spaggiari, Mladen Kovacevic, Brock Noland, and Ryan Bosshart

Published by O'Reilly Media, Inc., 1005 Gravenstein Highway North, Sebastopol, CA 95472.

O'Reilly books may be purchased for educational, business, or sales promotional use. Online editions are also available for most titles (*http://oreilly.com/safari*). For more information, contact our corporate/institutional sales department: 800-998-9938 or *corporate@oreilly.com*.

Editor: Nicole Tache
Production Editor: Colleen Cole
Copyeditor: Dwight Ramsey
Proofreaders: Charles Roumeliotis and Octal Publishing, Inc.
Indexer: Judy McConville

Interior Designer: David Futato
Cover Designer: Randy Comer
Illustrator: Melanie Yarbrough
Technical Reviewers: David Yahalom, Andy Stadtler, Attila Bukor, and Peter Paton

July 2018:   First Edition

Revision History for the First Edition
2018-07-09:   First Release

See *http://oreilly.com/catalog/errata.csp?isbn=9781491980255* for release details.

978-1-491-98025-5

[LSI]

To all those data people who day-in and day-out lead hair-pulling, brain-teasing, late-night lives architecting, developing, or consulting on software that appears to have gone rogue and deliberately misbehaves.

To our families, who may not even care about technology, yet still allowed us to give up time and energy to dedicate to this project with an enormous amount of patience and support, without which none of this was possible. We love you!

Table of Contents

Preface

Choosing a storage engine is one of the most important decisions anyone embarking on a big data project makes and is one of the most expensive to change. Apache Kudu is an entirely new storage manager for the Hadoop ecosystem. Its flexibility makes applications faster to build and easier to maintain. As a Hadoop developer, Kudu is a critical skill in your big data toolbox. It addresses common problems in big data that are difficult or impossible to implement on current generation Hadoop storage technologies.

In this book, you will learn key concepts of Kudu's design and how to architect applications against it, resulting in Kudu applications that are fast, scalable, and reliable. Through hands-on examples, you will learn how Kudu integrates with other Hadoop ecosystem components like Apache Spark, SparkSQL, and Impala.

This book assumes some limited experience with Hadoop ecosystem components like HDFS, Hive, Spark, or Impala. Basic programming experience using Java and/or Scala, experience with SQL and traditional RDBMS systems, and familiarity with the Linux shell is also assumed.

Conventions Used in This Book

The following typographical conventions are used in this book:

Italic
: Indicates new terms, URLs, email addresses, filenames, and file extensions.

`Constant width`
: Used for program listings, as well as within paragraphs to refer to program elements such as variable or function names, databases, data types, environment variables, statements, and keywords.

`Constant width bold`
: Shows commands or other text that should be typed literally by the user.

Constant width italic

Shows text that should be replaced with user-supplied values or by values determined by context.

This element signifies a tip or suggestion.

This element signifies a general note.

This element indicates a warning or caution.

Using Code Examples

Supplemental material (code examples, exercises, etc.) is available for download at *https://github.com/kudu-book/getting-started-kudu*.

This book is here to help you get your job done. In general, if example code is offered with this book, you may use it in your programs and documentation. You do not need to contact us for permission unless you're reproducing a significant portion of the code. For example, writing a program that uses several chunks of code from this book does not require permission. Selling or distributing a CD-ROM of examples from O'Reilly books does require permission. Answering a question by citing this book and quoting example code does not require permission. Incorporating a significant amount of example code from this book into your product's documentation does require permission.

We appreciate, but do not require, attribution. An attribution usually includes the title, author, publisher, and ISBN. For example: "*Getting Started with Kudu* by Jean-Marc Spaggiari, Mladen Kovacevic, Brock Noland, Ryan Bosshart (O'Reilly). Copyright 2018 Jean-Marc Spaggiari, Mladen Kovacevic, Brock Noland, Ryan Bosshart, 978-1-491-98025-5."

If you feel your use of code examples falls outside fair use or the permission given above, feel free to contact us at *permissions@oreilly.com*.

O'Reilly Safari

 *Safari* (formerly Safari Books Online) is a membership-based training and reference platform for enterprise, government, educators, and individuals.

Members have access to thousands of books, training videos, Learning Paths, interactive tutorials, and curated playlists from over 250 publishers, including O'Reilly Media, Harvard Business Review, Prentice Hall Professional, Addison-Wesley Professional, Microsoft Press, Sams, Que, Peachpit Press, Adobe, Focal Press, Cisco Press, John Wiley & Sons, Syngress, Morgan Kaufmann, IBM Redbooks, Packt, Adobe Press, FT Press, Apress, Manning, New Riders, McGraw-Hill, Jones & Bartlett, and Course Technology, among others.

For more information, please visit *http://oreilly.com/safari*.

How to Contact Us

Please address comments and questions concerning this book to the publisher:

O'Reilly Media, Inc.
1005 Gravenstein Highway North
Sebastopol, CA 95472
800-998-9938 (in the United States or Canada)
707-829-0515 (international or local)
707-829-0104 (fax)

We have a web page for this book, where we list errata, examples, and any additional information. You can access this page at *http://bit.ly/getting-started-with-kudu*.

To comment or ask technical questions about this book, send email to *bookquestions@oreilly.com*.

For more information about our books, courses, conferences, and news, see our website at *http://www.oreilly.com*.

Find us on Facebook: *http://facebook.com/oreilly*

Follow us on Twitter: *http://twitter.com/oreillymedia*

Watch us on YouTube: *http://www.youtube.com/oreillymedia*

Acknowledgments

We would like to thank the people of the Apache Kudu community for their help. This includes the creators, committers, contributors, early adopters, and users of Apache Kudu. Thank you to our technical reviewers David Yahalom, Andy Stadtler, and Attila Bukor for their careful attention to detail and feedback. Thank you to the unofficial technical reviewers as well, including Nipun Parasrampuria, Mac Noland, Sandish Kumar, Tony Foerster, Mike Rasmussen, Jordan Birdsell, and Gunaranjan Sundararajan.

Ryan Bosshart and Brock Noland would like to thank their colleagues at phData and Cloudera for their support and input in this book.

Mladen Kovacevic would like to thank his Cloudera colleagues who include solutions architects, engineers, support, product management, and others for the enthusiasm and support. Mladen is likewise grateful to his family for their patience, support, and encouragement while writing—it could not have been done without them!

Jean-Marc Spaggiari would like to thank everyone who supported him over this experience.

## CHAPTER 1

Why Kudu?

Why Does Kudu Matter?

As big data platforms continue to innovate and evolve, whether on-premises or in the cloud, it's no surprise that many are feeling some fatigue at the pace of new open source big data project releases. After working with Kudu for the past year with large companies and real-world use cases, we're more convinced than ever that Kudu matters and that it's very much worthwhile to add yet another project to the open source big data world.

Our reasoning boils down to three essential points:

1. Big data is still too difficult—as the audience and appetite for data grows, Hadoop and big data platforms are still too difficult, and much of this complexity is driven from limitations in storage. At our office, long-winded architecture discussions are now being cut short with the common refrain, "Just use Kudu and be done with it."

2. New use cases need Kudu—the use cases Hadoop is being called upon to serve are changing—this includes an increasing focus on machine-generated data and real-time analytics. To demonstrate this complexity, we walk through some architectures for real-time analytics using existing big data storage technologies and discuss how Kudu simplifies these architectures.

3. The hardware landscape is changing—many of the fundamental assumptions about hardware upon which Hadoop was built are changing. There are fresh opportunities to create a storage manager with improved performance and workload flexibility.

In this chapter we discuss the aforementioned motivations in detail. If you're already familiar with the motivation for Kudu, you can skip to the latter part of this chapter where we discuss some of Kudu's goals and how Kudu compares to other big data storage systems. We finish up by summarizing why the world needs another big data storage system.

Simplicity Drives Adoption

Distributed systems used to be expensive and difficult. We worked for a large media and information provider in the mid-2000s building a platform for the ingest, processing, search, storage, and retrieval of hundreds of terabytes of online content. Building such a platform was a gargantuan effort involving hundreds of engineers and teams dedicated to building different parts of the platform. We had separate teams dedicated to distributed systems for ingest, storage, search, content retrieval, and so on. To scale our platform, we sharded our relational stores, search indexes, and storage systems and then built elaborate metadata systems on top in order to keep everything sorted out. The platform was built on expensive proprietary technologies that acted as a barrier to ward off smaller competing companies wanting to do the same thing.

Around the same time, Doug Cutting and Mike Carafella were building Apache Hadoop. Thanks to their work and the work of the entire Hadoop ecosystem community, building scale-out infrastructure no longer requires many millions of dollars and huge teams of specialized distributed systems engineers. One of Hadoop's first advancements was that a software engineer with very modest knowledge of distributed systems had access to scale-out data platforms. It made distributed computing for the software engineer easier.

Although the software engineers rejoiced, that was just a slice of the total population of people wanting access to big data. Hence, the church of big data continued to grow and diversify. Starting with Hive, and then Impala, and then all the other SQL-on-Hadoop engines, analysts and SQL engineers with no programming background have been able to process and analyze their data at scale using Hadoop. By providing a familiar interface, SQL has allowed a huge group of users waiting on the doorstep of Hadoop to be let in. SQL-on-Hadoop mattered because it made data processing and analysis easier and faster versus a programming language. That's not to say that SQL made Hadoop "easy." Ask anyone coming from the relational database management system (RDBMS) world and they will tell you that even though SQL certainly made Hadoop more usable, there are plenty of gaps and caveats to watch out for. In addition, especially in the early days, engineers and analysts needed to decide which specific engine or format best fit their particular use case. We talk about the specific challenges later in this chapter, but for now, let's say that SQL-on-Hadoop made distributed computing easy for the SQL-savvy data engineer.

At the time of this writing, Hive Kudu support is still pending in HIVE-12971 (*https://issues.apache.org/jira/browse/HIVE-12971*). However, it's still possible to create *Hive* tables, which Impala accesses.

More users want in on this scalable goodness. With the rise of machine learning and data science, big data platforms are now serving statisticians, mathematicians, and a broader audience of data analysts. Productivity for these users is driven by fast iteration and performance. The effectiveness of the data scientist's model is often driven by data volume, making Hadoop an obvious choice. These users are familiar with SQL but are not "engineers" and therefore not interested in dealing with some of Hadoop's nuances. They expect even better usability, simplicity, and performance.

In addition, traditional enterprise business intelligence and analytics systems people also want in on the Hadoop action, leading to even more demand for performant and mature SQL systems.

Hadoop democratized big data, both technically and econimically, and made it possible for a programmer or software engineer with little knowledge of the intricacies of distributed systems to ingest, store, process, and serve huge amounts of data. Over time, Hadoop has evolved further and can now serve an even broader audience of users. As a result, we've all been witness to a fairly obvious fact: the easier a data platform is to use, the more adoption it will gain, the more users it can serve, and the more value it can provide. This has certainly been true of Hadoop over the past 10 years. As Hadoop became simpler and easier to use, we've seen increased adoption and value (Figure 1-1).

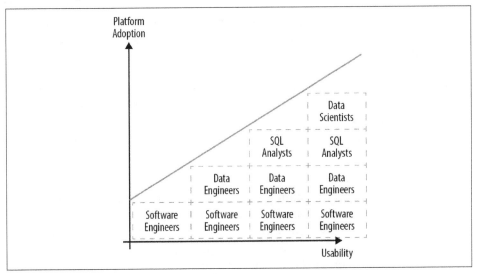

Figure 1-1. Hadoop adoption and simplicity

Kudu's simplicity grows Hadoop's "addressable market." It does this by providing functionality and a data model closer to what you'd see in an RDBMS. Kudu provides a relational-like table construct for storing data and allows users to insert, update, and delete data, in much the same way that you can with a relational database. This model is familiar to just about everyone who interacts with data—software engineers, analysts, Extract, Transfer, and Load (ETL) developers, data scientists, statisticians, and so on. In addition, it also aligns with the use cases that Hadoop is being asked to solve today.

New Use Cases

Hadoop is being stretched in terms of the use cases it's being expected to solve. These use cases are driven by the combined force of several factors. One is the macro-trends of data, like the rise of real-time analytics and the Internet of Things (IoT). These workloads are complex to design properly and can be a brick wall for even experienced Hadoop developers. Another factor is the changing user audience of the platform, as discussed in the previous section. With new users come new use cases and new ways to use the platform. Another factor is increasing expectations of end users of data. Five to ten years ago, batch was okay. After all, we couldn't even process this much data before! But today, being able to scalably store and process data is table stakes; users expect real-time results and speedy performance for a variety of workloads.

Let's look at some of these use cases and the demands they place on storage.

IoT

By 2020, there are projected to be 20 to 30 billion connected devices in the world. These devices come in every shape and form you can imagine. There are massive "connected cargo and passenger ships" instrumented with sensors monitoring everything from fuel consumption to engines and location. There are now connected cars, connected mining equipment, and connected refrigerators. Implanted medical devices responsible for delivering life-saving therapies like pacing, defibrillation, and neuro-stimulation are now able to emit data that can be used to recognize when a patient is having a medical episode or when there are issues with a device that needs maintenance or replacement.

Billions of connected devices creates an obvious scale problem and makes Hadoop a good choice, but the precise architectural solution is less obvious than you might at first think. Suppose that we have a connected medical device and we want to analyze data from that device. Let's begin with a simple set of requirements: we want to be able to stream events from connected devices into a storage layer, whatever that might be, and then be able to query the data in just a couple ways. First, we want to be able to see what's happening with the device right now. For example, after rolling out a software update to our device, we want to be able look at up-to-the-second signals coming off the device to understand if our update is having the desired effect or encountering any issues. The other access pattern is analytics; we have data analysts who are looking for trends in data to gain new insights to understand and report on device performance, studying, for example, things like battery usage and optimization.

To serve these basic access patterns (Figure 1-2), the storage layer needs the following capabilities:

Row-by-row inserts

When the application server or gateway device receives an event, it needs to be able to save that event to storage, making it immediately available for readers.

Low-latency random reads

After deploying an update to some devices, it needs to analyze the performance of a subset of devices and time. This means being able to efficiently look up a small range of rows.

Fast analytical scans

To serve reporting and ad hoc analytics needs, we need to be able to scan large volumes of data efficiently from storage.

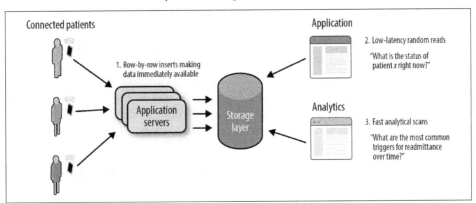

Figure 1-2. IoT access patterns

Current Approaches to Real-Time Analytics

Let's take a look at a simple example of what's required to successfully implement a real-time streaming analytics use case without Kudu.

In this example, we have a data source producing continuous streams of events (Figure 1-3). We need to store these events in near real time, as our users require these events to be made available to them, because the value of this data is highest when it's first created. The architecture consists of a producer that takes events from the source and then saves them to some yet-to-be-determined storage layer so that the events can be analyzed by business users via SQL, and data scientists and developers using Spark. The concept of the producer is generic; it could be a Flume agent, SparkStreaming job, or a standalone application.

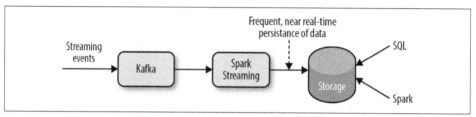

Figure 1-3. Simple real-time analytics flow

Choosing a storage engine for this use case is a surprisingly thorny decision. Let's take a look at our options using traditional Hadoop storage engines.

Iteration 1: Hadoop Distributed File System

In our first iteration, we're going to try to keep things simple and save our data in Hadoop Distributed File System (HDFS) as Avro files. While we're picking on HDFS in this example, these same principles apply when using other storage layers like Amazon Web Services Simple Storage Service (Amazon S3). Avro is a row-based data format. Row-based formats work well with streaming systems because large numbers of rows need to be buffered in memory when writing columnar formats such as Parquet. We create a Hive table, partitioned by date, and from our producer, write microbatches of data as Avro files in HDFS. Because users want access to data soon after creation, the producer is frequently writing new files to HDFS. For example, if our producer were a Spark Streaming application running a micro-batch every 10 seconds, the application would also save a new batch every 10 seconds in order to make the data available to consumers.

We deploy our new system to the production cluster. The high-level data flow now looks like Figure 1-4.

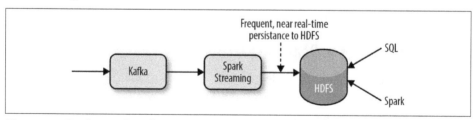

Figure 1-4. Real-time data flow using HDFS

A couple days after deploying the application, the tickets begin flowing. The Operations Team is receiving user reports that performance is slow and their jobs won't complete. After looking into some of the jobs, we see that our HDFS directory has tens of thousands of tiny files. As it turns out, each of these tiny files ends up requiring HDFS to do a disk seek and destroys the performance of Spark jobs and Impala queries. Unfortunately, the only way to solve this issue is by reducing the number of small files, which is what we do next.

Iteration 2: HDFS + Compactions

After some googling, we find out this is a problem with a well-known solution: adding an HDFS compaction process (*https://blog.cloudera.com/blog/2015/11/how-to-ingest-and-query-fast-data-with-impala-without-kudu/*). The previously mentioned parts of the architecture remain mostly in place; however, because the ingestion process is rapidly creating small files, there is a new offline compaction process. The compaction process takes the many small files and rewrites them into a smaller number of large files. Although the solution seems easy enough, there are a number of complicating factors. For example, the compaction process will run over a partition after it's no longer active. That compaction process can't overwrite results into that same partition or you'll momentarily lose data and active queries can fail. You could write the result into a separate location and then switch them out using HDFS commands, but even then, two HDFS commands are required and consistency cannot be achieved.

The complications don't stop there. The final HDFS-based solution ends up requiring two separate "landing" directories in HDFS: an active version and a passive version, and a "base" directory for compacted data. The architecture now looks like Figure 1-5 (courtesy of the Cloudera Engineering Blog).

This architecture contains multiple HDFS directories, multiple Hive/Impala tables, and several views. Developers must create orchestration to switch writers between the two active/passive landing directories, use the compaction process to move data from "landing" to "base" tables, modify the tables and metadata with the new compacted partitions, clean up the old data, and utilize several view modifications to ensure readers are able to see consistent data.

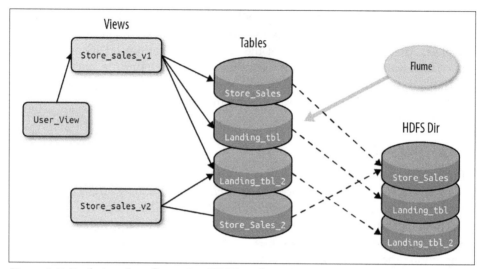

Figure 1-5. Real-time data flow using HDFS with compactions

Even though you've created an architecture capable of handling large-scale data with lower latency, the solution still has many compromises. For one, the solution is still only pseudo "real time." This is because there are still small files, just fewer of them. The more frequently data is written to HDFS, the greater the number of small files, and the efficiency of processing jobs plummets, leading to lower cluster efficiency and job performance. As a result, you might write results to disk only once per minute, so calling this architecture "real time" requires a broad definition of the term. In addition, because HDFS has no notion of a primary key and many stream processing systems have the potential to produce duplicates (i.e., at-least-once versus at-most-once semantics), we need a mechanism that we can use for de-duplication. The result is that our compaction process and table views need to also do de-duplication. Finally, if we have late arriving data, it will not fall within the current day's compaction and will result in more small files.

Iteration 3: HBase + HDFS

The complexity and shortcomings mentioned in the previous examples come mostly as a result of trying to get HDFS to do things for which it wasn't optimized or designed. There is yet another and perhaps better-known option in which instead of trying to optimize a single storage layer for nonoptimal performance and usage characteristics, we can marry two storage layers based on their respective strengths. This idea is similar to the Lambda architecture in which you have a "speed layer" and a "batch layer." The speed layer ingests streaming data and provides storage capable of point lookups on recent data, mutability, and crucially, low-latency reads and writes. For clients needing an up-to-the-second view of the data, the speed layer makes this data available. The traditional Hadoop options for the speed layer are HBase or its "big table" cousin Cassandra. HBase and Cassandra thrive in online, real-time, highly concurrent environments; however, their Achilles' heel is that they do not provide the fast analytical scan performance of HDFS and Parquet. Thus, to enable fast scans and analytics, you must shift data out of speed layer and into the batch layer of HDFS and Parquet.

Data is now being streamed into our speed layer of HBase or Cassandra. When "enough" data has accumulated, a flusher process comes along and moves data from the speed layer to the batch layer. Usually this is done after enough data has accumulated in the speed layer to fill an HDFS partition, so the flusher process is responsible for reading data from the speed layer, rewriting it as Parquet, adding a new partition to HDFS, and then alerting Hive and Impala of the new partition. Because data is now stored in two separate storage managers, clients for this data either need to be aware of the data being in two places, or you must add a service layer to stitch the two layers together to abstract users from this detail. In the end, our architecture looks something like that shown in Figure 1-6.

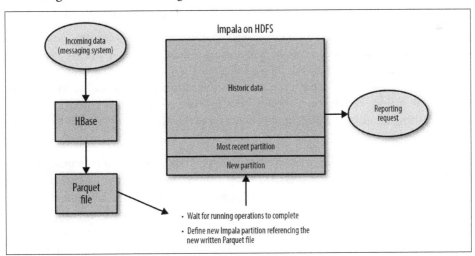

Figure 1-6. Real time data flow using HBase and HDFS

This architecture represents a scale-out solution with the advantages of fresh, up-to-the-second data, mutability, and fast scans. However, it fails when it comes to simplicity of development, operations, and maintenance. Developers are tasked with developing and maintaining code for not only data ingest, but the flusher process to move data out of the speed layer into the batch layer. Operators must now maintain another storage manager, if they aren't already, and must monitor, maintain, and troubleshoot processes for both data ingestion and the process to move data from the speed layer to the batch layer. Lastly, with new and historical data spread between two storage managers, there isn't an easy way for clients to get a unified view from both the speed and batch layers.

These approaches are sophisticated solutions to a seemingly simple problem: scalable, up-to-the-second analytics on rapidly produced data. These solutions aren't easily developed, maintained, or operated. As a result, they tend to be implemented only for use cases in which the value is sure to justify the high level of effort. It is our observation that, due to this complexity, the aforementioned solutions see limited adoption and, in most cases, users settle for a simpler, batch-based solution.

Real-Time Processing

Scalable stream processing is another trend gaining steam in the Hadoop ecosystem. As evidence, you can just look at the number of projects and companies building products in this space. The idea behind stream processing is that rather than saving data to storage and processing the data in batches afterward, events are processed in flight. Unlike batch processing in which there is a defined beginning and end of a batch, in stream processing, the processor is long-lived and operates constantly on small batches of events as they arrive. Stream processing is often used to look at data and make immediate decisions on how to transform, aggregate, filter, or alert on data.

Real-time processing can be useful in model scoring, complex event processing, data enrichment, or many other types of processing. These types of patterns apply in a variety of domains for which the "time-value" of the data is high, meaning that the data is most valuable soon after creation and then diminishes thereafter. Many types of fraud detection, healthcare analytics, and IoT use cases fit this pattern. A major factor limiting adoption of real-time processing is the challenging demands it places on data storage.

Stream processing often requires external context. That context can take many different forms. In some cases, you need historical context and you want to know how the recent data compares to data points in history. In other cases, referential data is required. Fraud detection, for example, relies heavily on both historical and referential data. Historical data will include features like the number of transactions in the past 24 hours or the past week. Referential features might include things like a customer's account information or the location of an IP address.

Although processing frameworks like Apache Flume, Storm, SparkStreaming, and Flink provide the ability to read and process events in real time, they rely on external systems for storage and access of external context. For example, when using Spark-Streaming, you could read micro-batches of events from Kafka every few seconds. If you wanted to be able to save results, read external context, calculate a risk score, and update a patient profile, you now have a diverse set of storage demands:

Row-by-row inserts
As events are being generated, they need to be immediately saved and available for analysis by other tools or processes.

Low-latency random reads

When a streaming engine encounters an event, it might need to look up specific reference information related to that event. For example, if the event represents data from a medical device, specific contextual information about the patient might be needed, such as the name of their clinic or particular information related to their condition.

Fast analytical scans

How does this event relate to history? Being able to run fast analytical scans and SQL in order to gain historical context is often important.

Updates

Contextual information can change. For example, contextual information being fed from Online Transactional Processing (OLTP) applications might populate reference data like contact information, or a patient's risk score might be updated as new information is computed.

When examining these use cases, you've surely noticed the theme of having "real-time" capabilities. And you might correctly point out that many organizations are successfully accomplishing the use cases we just mentioned on Hadoop without Kudu. This is true; taken separately, the Hadoop storage layers can handle fast inserts, low-latency random reads, updates, and fast scans. Low-latency reads and writes of your data, yep, got HBase for that. Fast analytics? HDFS can scan your data like nobody's business—what else you got? Looking for something simple to use? Sure, we can batch ingest your files into HDFS with one command! The trouble comes when you ask for all those things: row-by-row inserts, random-reads, fast scan, and updates —all in one. This leads to complex, often difficult to maintain architectures as demonstrated in Figure 1-7.

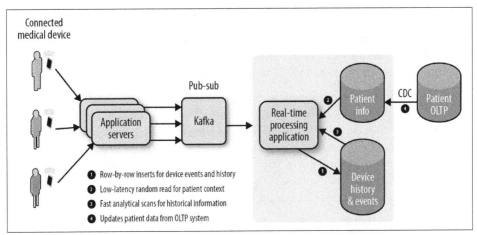

Figure 1-7. Real-time data flow

Handling this diverse list of storage characteristics is possible in many relational databases but immensely difficult using Hadoop and big data. The brutal reality of Hadoop is that these use cases are difficult because the platform forces you to choose storage layers based on a subset of these characterstics.

Hardware Landscape

Hadoop was designed with specific hardware performance and cost considerations in mind. If we go back 15 or so years, when the ideas for Hadoop originated, a reasonably priced server contained some CPU, let's say 8 or 16 GB of DRAM, and exclusively spinning disks. Hadoop was ingeniously designed to maximize cost and performance, minimizing the use of expensive DRAM and avoiding precious disk seeks to maximize throughput. The steady march of Moore's Law has ensured that more bits can fit on our memory chips as well. Commodity servers now have several hundreds of gigabytes of DRAM, tens of terabytes of disk, and increasingly, new types of nonvolatile storage.

This brings us to one of the most dramatic changes happening in hardware today. An average server today is increasingly likely to contain some solid-state, or NAND, storage, which brings new potential. Solid-state drive (SSD) storage brings huge changes in performance characteristics and the removal of many traditional bottlenecks in computing. Specifically, NAND-based storage can handle more I/O, is capable of throughput, and has lower latency seeks versus the traditional hard-disk drive (HDD). Newer trends like three-dimensional NAND strorage are exaggerating these performance changes even further. An L1 cache reference takes about half a nanosecond, DRAM is about 200 nanoseconds, 3D-XPoint (3D NAND from Intel (*http:// bit.ly/2zpI1hu*)) takes about 7,000 nanoseconds, an SSD drive around 100,000 nanoseconds, and a disk seek is 10 million nanoseconds. To understand the scale of the performance difference between these mediums, suppose that the L1 cache reference is one second. In equivalent terms, a DRAM read would be about six minutes, 3D NAND (3D XPoint, in this case) would be around four hours, an SSD would be a little more than two days, and an HDD seek would be around seven months.

Speed and performance have profound implications on system design. Think about how the speed of transport enabled by automobiles reshaped the world's cities and suburbs in the 20th century. With the birth of the car, people were suddenly able to live further away from city centers while still having access to the ammenities and services of a city via automobile. Cities sparawled and suburbs were born. However, with all these fast cars on the road, a new bottleneck arose, and suddenly there was traffic! As a result of all the fast cars, we had to create larger and more efficient roads.

In the context of Hadoop and Kudu, the shift to NAND storage dramatically lowers the computational cost of a disk seek, meaning a storage system can do more of them. If you're using SSD for storage, you expect to be able to reasonably serve new workloads with random read/write for increased flexibility. SSDs also bring improvements in Input/output operations per second (IOPS) and throughput, so as data is being brought to the CPU more efficiently, this sets up the potential for a new bottleneck—the CPU. As we look further into the future and these trends are further exaggerated, data platforms should be able to take advantage of improved random I/O performance and should be CPU efficient.

As you might expect, if you purchase one (or one thousand) of these servers, you expect your software to be able to fully utilize its advantages. Practically speaking, this means that if your servers now have hundreds of gigabytes of RAM, you are able to scale your heap to serve more data from memory and see reduced latency.

The hardware landscape continues to evolve and the bottlenecks, cost considerations, and performance of hardware are vastly different today than they were 20 years ago when the ideas behind Hadoop first began. These trends continue to and will continue to change rapidly.

Kudu's Unique Place in the Big Data Ecosystem

Like other parts of Hadoop, Kudu is designed to be scalable and fault tolerant. Kudu is explicitly a storage layer; therefore, it is not meant to process data and instead relies on the external processing engines of Hadoop, like MapReduce, Spark, or Impala, for that functionality. Although it integrates with many Hadoop components, Kudu can also run as a self-contained, standalone storage engine and does not depend on other frameworks like HDFS or Zookeeper. Kudu stores data in its own columnar format natively in the underlying Linux filesystem and does not utilize HDFS in any way, unlike HBase, for instance.

Kudu's data model will be familiar to anyone coming from an RDBMS background. Even though Kudu is not a SQL engine itself, its data model is similar to that of a database. Tables are created with a fixed number of typed columns, and a subset of those columns will make up your primary key. As in an RDBMS, the primary key enforces uniqueness for that row. Kudu utilizes a columnar format on disk; this enables efficient encoding and fast scans on a subset of columns. To achieve scale and fault-tolerance, Kudu tables are broken up into horizontal chunks, called *tablets*, and writes are replicated among tablets using a consensus algorithm, called *Raft*.

Kudu's design is fueled by a keen understanding of complex architectures and limitations in present-day Hadoop as well as stark difference developers and architects have to make when choosing a storage engine. Kudu acts as a moderate choice with the goal of having a strong breadth of capabilities and good performance for a variety of workloads. Specifically, Kudu blends low-latency random access, row-by-row inserts, updates, and fast analytical scans into a single storage layer. As discussed, venerable storage engines of HDFS, HBase, and Cassandra have each of these capabilities in isolation; none have all of these capabilities themselves. This difference in workload characteristics between existing Hadoop storage engines is referred to as the *analytical gap* and is illustrated in Figure 1-8.

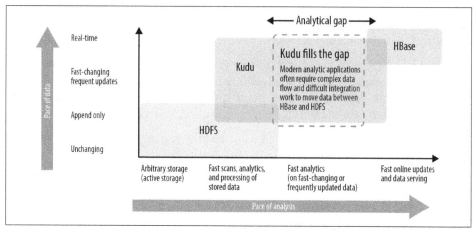

Figure 1-8. Kudu fills the storage gap

HDFS is an append-only filesystem; it performs best with large files for which a processing engine can scan huge amounts of data sequentially. On the other end of the spectrum is Apache HBase or its big table cousins like Cassandra. HBase and Cassandra brought real-time reads and writes and other features needed for online OLTP-like workloads. HBase thrives in online, real-time, highly concurrent environments with mostly random reads and writes or short scans.

You'll notice in the illustration that Kudu doesn't claim to be faster than HBase or HDFS for any one particular workload. Kudu has high throughput scans and is fast for analytics. Kudu's goal is to be within two times of HDFS with Parquet or ORCFile for scan performance. Like HBase, Kudu has fast, random reads and writes for point lookups and updates, with the goal of one millisecond read/write latencies on SSD.

If we revisit our earlier real-time analytics use case, this time using Kudu, you'll notice that our architecture is dramatically simpler (Figure 1-9). The first thing to note is that there is a single storage and there are not user-initiated compactions or storage optimization processes. For the operators, they have only one system to monitor and maintain, and they don't need to mess with cron jobs to shuffle data between speed and batch layers, or among Hive partitions. Developers don't need to deal with writing data maintenance code or handle special cases for late arriving data, and updates are handled with ease. For the users, they have immediate access to their real-time and historical data, all in one place.

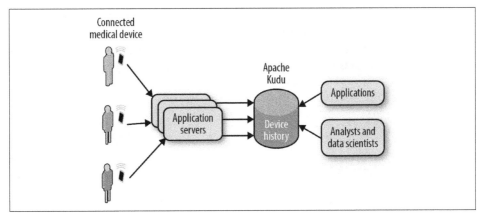

Figure 1-9. Architecture with Kudu

Comparing Kudu with Other Ecosystem Components

Kudu is a new storage system. With the hundreds of databases that have been created over the past 10 years, we personally feel fatigued. Why another storage system? In this section, we continue to answer that question by comparing Kudu against the landscape of traditional ecosystem components.

The easiest comparison is with the SQL engines such as Hive, Impala, and SparkSQL. Kudu doesn't execute SQL queries in whole. There are parts of the SQL query that can be pushed down to the storage layer, such as projection and predicates, which are indeed executed in Kudu. However, a SQL engine has parsers, a planner, and a method for executing the queries. Kudu functions only during query execution and provides input to the planner. Furthermore, Kudu must have projection and predicates pushed down or communicated to it by the SQL engine to participate in the execution of the query and act as more than a simple storage engine.

Now let's compare Kudu against a traditional relational database. To discuss this, we need to define the types of relational databases. Broadly speaking, there are two kinds of relational databases, Online Transactional Processing (OLTP) and Online Analytical Processing (OLAP) (Figure 1-10). OLTP databases are used for online services on websites, point of sale (PoS), and other applications for which users expect immediate response and strong data integrity. However, typically OLTP databases do not perform well at large scans, which are common in analytical workloads. For example, when servicing a website, an orders page will commonly display all orders for a particular user, e.g., "My Orders" on any online website. However in an analytical context you typically don't care about orders for a particular user, you care about all sales of a given product and often all sales of a particular provider grouped by, for instance, state. OLAP databases perform these types of queries well because they are optimized for scans. Typically, OLAP databases perform poorly at the types of use cases for which OLTP databases are good ; for example, selects of a small number of rows and commonly integrity. You might be surprised that any database would sacrifice on integrity, but OLAP databases are typically loaded in batches, so if anything goes wrong, the entire batch is reloaded without any data loss.

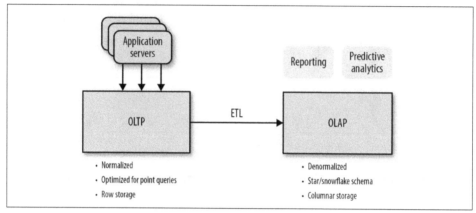

Figure 1-10. OLTP and OLAP

There is another concept we must be aware of before proceeding. Rows of data can be stored in row or column format (see Figures 1-11 and 1-12). Typically, OLTP databases use row format, whereas OLAP databases use columnar. Row formats are great for full-row retreivals and updates. Columnar formats are great for large scans that select a subset of the columns. A typical OLTP query is to get the full row, whereas a typical OLAP query retrieves only part of the row.

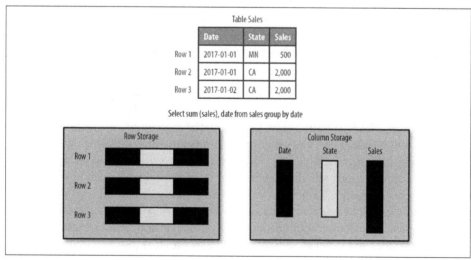

Figure 1-11. Row and column storage, part 1

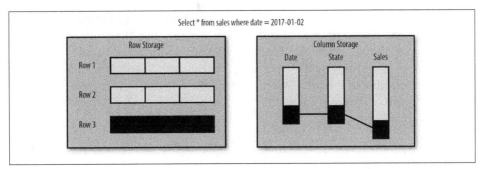

Figure 1-12. Row and column storage, part 2

Not to beat a dead horse, but if you imagine a "My Orders" page on an online store, you will see all relevant information about the order including the billing and shipping addresses along with product name, code, quantity, and price. However, for a query that calculates total sales for a given product by state, the only fields of interest are the product name, quantity, price, and billing state.

Now that we have defined OLTP and OLAP along with row and column format, we can finally compare Kudu versus relational database systems. Today, Kudu is most often thought of as a columnar storage engine for OLAP SQL query engines Hive, Impala, and SparkSQL. However, because rows can be quickly retrieved by primary key and continuously ingested all while the table is being scanned for analytical queries, Kudu has some properties of both OLTP and OLAP systems, putting it in a third category that we discuss later.

There are many, many kinds of relational databases in both the OLTP and OLAP spaces ranging from single process databases such SQLite (OLTP) to shared everything partitioned databases such as Oracle RAC (OLTP/OLAP) to shared nothing partitioned databases such as MySQL Cluster (OLTP) and Vertica (OLAP). Kudu has much in common with relational databases; for example, Kudu tables have a unique primary key, unlike HBase and Cassandra. However, features that are common in relational databases such as common types of transactional support, foreign keys, and nonprimary key indexes are not supported in Kudu. These are all possible and on the roadmap, but not yet implemented.

Kudu plus Impala is most similar to Vertica. Vertica is a postgres variation using storage based on a system called C-Store (*http://cs-www.cs.yale.edu/homes/dna/papers/ vldb.pdf*) from which Kudu also takes some heritage. However, there are important differences. First, because the Hadoop ecosystem is not vertically integrated liked traditional databases, we can bring many query engines to the same storage systems. Second, because Kudu implemented a quorum-based storage system, it has stronger durability guarantees. Third, because Hadoop-based query engines schedule work where data resides locally, as opposed to using a shared storage system such as SAN, queries benefit from what is known as *data locality*. Data locality just means that the "work" can read data from a local disk, which typically has less contention than a shared storage device. Some databases like Vertica, which are based on shared-nothing design, can also schedule work "close" to the data. But they can schedule only Vertica queries, close to the data. You can extend them to add new engines and work-loads on account of their vertically integrated nature.

Kudu today has some OLAP and OLTP characteristics minus cross-row Atomicity, Consistency, Isolation, Durability (ACID) transactions, putting it in a category known as Hybrid Transactional/Analytic Processing (HTAP). For example, Kudu was built to allow for fast record retrieval by primary key and continuous ingest along with constant analytics. OLAP databases don't often perform well with this mix of use cases. Additionally, Kudu's durability guarantees are closer to an OLTP database than OLAP. Long term, it can be even stronger with synchronous cross-datacenter replication similar to Google Spanner, an OLTP system. Kudu with its quorum capability has the ability to implement what is known as Fractured Mirrors (*http://www.vldb.org/conf/2002/S12P03.pdf*) in which one or two nodes in a quorum use a row format, whereas the third node stores data in a column format. This would allow you to schedule OLTP-style queries on row-format nodes, whereas you can perform OLAP queries on the columnar nodes, mixing both workloads. Lastly, the underlying hardware is changing, which also, given sufficient support, can blur the lines between these two kinds of databases. For example, a big problem when using a columnar database for an OLTP workload is that OLTP workloads often want to retrieve a large subset of a row; in a columnar database that can translate to many disk seeks. How-ever, SSD and persistent memory are mostly eliminating this problem.

Big Data—HDFS, HBase, Cassandra

With all this in mind, how does Kudu compare against other big data storage systems such as HDFS, HBase, and Cassandra? Let's define at a high level what these other systems do well. HDFS is extremely good when a program is scanning large volumes of data. In short, it's fantastic at "full-table scans," which are extremely common in analytical workloads. HBase and Cassandra are great at random access, reading or modifying data at random. HDFS is poor at random reads, and although it cannot technically perform random writes, you can simulate them through a merge process, which is expensive. HBase and Cassandra, on the other hand, perform extremely poorly relative to HDFS at large scans. Kudu's goal is to be within two times that of Parquet on HDFS for scans, and similarly close to HBase and Cassandra for random reads. The actual random read goal is one millisecond read/write on SSD.

We go into a little more detail on each system so as to describe why HDFS, HBase, Cassandra, and Kudu perform the way they do. HDFS is a purely distributed filesys-tem that was designed to perform fast, large scans. After all, the first use case for this design was to build an index of the web in batch. For that use case, and many others, you simply need to be able to scan the entire dataset in a performant manner. HDFS partitions data and spreads it out over a large number of physical disks so that these large scans can utilize many drives in parallel.

HBase and Cassandra are similar to Kudu in that they store data in rows and columns and provide the ability to randomly access the data. However, when it comes to storing data on disk, they store it much differently than Kudu. There are many reasons Kudu is faster at scanning data than these systems, but one of the major reasons is that HBase and Cassandra store data in column families; as such, they are not truly columnar. The net result is twofold: first, data cannot be encoded in columns, which results in extreme compression (as discussed later similar data stored "close" to each other compresses better) and second, one column in the family cannot be scanned without physically reading the other columns.

Another reason Kudu is faster for large scans is that it doesn't perform scan-time merges. Kudu doesn't guarantee that scans return data in exact primary key order (fine for most analytic use cases), and thus we don't need to perform any "merge" between different RowSets (chunks of rows). The "merge" in HBase happens for two reasons: to provide order, to allow new versions of cells or tombstones to *overwrite* earlier versions. We don't need the first because we don't guarantee order, and we don't need the second because we use an entirely different delta-tracking design. Rather than storing different versions of each cell, we store *base data*, and then separate blocks with *deltas* forward/backward from there. If you have had few recent updates, forward deltas get compacted into REDOs and only backward UNDOs are stored. Then, for a current-time query, we know that we can disregard all backward deltas, meaning that we need to read only the base data.

Reading the base data is very efficient because of its columnar and dense nature. Having schemas means that we don't need to encode column names or value lengths for each cell, and having the deltas segregated means that we don't need to look at timestamps either, resulting in a scan that is nearly as efficient as Parquet.

One particular reason for efficiency relative to HBase is that in avoiding all of these per-cell comparisons, we avoid a lot of CPU branch mispredictions. Each generation of CPUs over the past 10 years has had a deeper pipeline and thus a more expensive branch misprediction cost, and so we get a lot more "bang for the buck" per CPU cycle.

Conclusion

Kudu is neither appropriate for all situations nor will it completely replace venerable storage engines like HDFS or newer cloud storage like Amazon S3 or Microsoft Azure Data Lake Store. In addition, there are certainly use cases for HBase and Cassandra that Kudu cannot fill today. However, there is a strong wind in the market, and it's pushing data systems toward even greater scale, toward analytics, toward machine learning, and toward doing all of these things in an operational and real-time way—that is to say, production-scale, operational systems run machine learning and analytics to deliver a product or service to an end user. Being able to serve this blend of operational and analytical capabilities is the unique realm of Kudu. As we've demonstrated in this chapter, there are many ways to build such systems, but without Kudu, your architecture will likely be complex to develop and operate, and your data-sets might even be split between different storage engines.

## CHAPTER 2

About Kudu

Apache Kudu is often summarized in one single phrase: a Hadoop storage layer to enable fast analytics on fast data. Although a short, simple-to-understand statement, until now, achieving those goals has not been easy.

We can achieve analytics with today's big data technology. Namely, storing data in highly efficient, columnar storage formats in particular, such as Parquet and ORC, allows for compute engines to sequentially read data across the entire distributed file-system, HDFS, at a very high rate. Analytical type queries perform large aggregations over a subset of columns. This effectively translates to a projection of the columns the query is requesting coupled with performing a mathematical operation on a large number of values in that column. Thus, columnar storage formats are terrific because a) to project a column simply means you limit the I/O to solely the pages on disk containing data for that column—which is doable because the format is already split across columns, and b) numbers in particular can use various encoding and packing mechanisms to stuff massive amounts of data representing many rows onto a single page on disk. This means that I/O can be extremely efficient, and compute operations on the values in a column can be performed quickly. In short, the HDFS filesystem, coupled with columnar file formats, yields highly performant I/O and compute capability resulting in analytics queries being processed quickly.

On the other hand, we also can achieve fast data with today's big data technology. If we look at HBase, Cassandra, and other NoSQL storage engines, they are built from the ground up allowing data to come in and be stored at extremely high rates of ingestion, whether using bulk loads, or a whole set of put operations. They allow for effective INSERT (put()), UPDATE (put()), which will overwrite the existing record, or DELETE (delete()) operations for data given a particular unique key, and perform them at an extremely high rate. These engines typically have low response time for the scans, as well; however, that performance is limited to when scans are based on the key itself. Scanning through the dataset using any other column in these engines will result in poor performance given that only the key values are sorted and maintained. Performing lookups on specific keys is also extremely efficient in these storage engines, such as user or object profile information.

Table 2-1 compares different features between HBase, Parquet on HDFS, and Kudu.

Table 2-1. Storage layers comparison

Engine	Single row access	Transactions	Consistency	Random operations	Columnar	Compression	Key encoding	Data encoding
HBase	Yes	No	Row-level	Yes	Yes	Yes	Yes	No
Parquet	No	No	Partition	No	Yes	Yes	Yes	Yes
Kudu	Yes	No	Configurable[a]	Yes	Yes	Yes	Yes	Yes

[a] *https://kudu.apache.org/2017/09/18/kudu-consistency-pt1.html*

What we find then is that we can achieve both "fast analytics" as well as "fast data" in the Hadoop ecosystem today, but the key is that we cannot achieve it by a single storage engine. You can perform "fast analytics" at the cost of "slow data," whereas you can achieve "fast data" at the cost of "slow analytics."

Kudu's design goals from the very beginning were to provide a new storage layer founded on the idea of achieving both fast analytics and handling fast data so that the time from when data is generated and stored in Hadoop to the time data is served in providing analytics is shortened and simplified in a single storage engine.

Kudu has the properties of a columnar storage as found in typical storage file formats such as Parquet and ORC on HDFS, storing its data in a Parquet-like format, though no longer using HDFS as the underlying filesystem. It provides the user with a set of NoSQL-like APIs, such as `put`, `get`, `delete`, and `scan`, resembling a NoSQL engine such as HBase.

Finally, to coincide with the theme of big data in terms of high availability and resiliency to failures, Kudu employs several architectural measures to ensure high availability, resiliency, durability, and scalability to fit right in with the rest of the ecosystem.

Kudu High-Level Design

As we observed in Chapter 1, Kudu has been designed to achieve several master objectives:

- Allow users to scan data as fast as possible, up to twice the speed of scanning raw file access in HDFS

- Allow users to perform random reads and writes as fast as possible, with approximately one millisecond response times
- Do so in a highly available, fault-tolerant, durable fashion

To achieve those objectives, Kudu provides an architecture to perform extremely fast and scalable columnar storage and access to your data, with a truly distributed and fault-tolerant model. It is designed around today's next-generation hardware becoming readily available, taking advantage of the properties of the fastest solid-state drives (SSDs), Streaming SIMD Extensions 4 (SSE4), and Advanced Vector Extensions (AVX) instruction sets.

Kudu Roles

Kudu developed as a result of learning from numerous software projects already existing in the big data space. Several concepts are derived from BigTable (open source derivative HBase), GFS (open source derivative HDFS), Cassandra, and more, somewhat taking the "best of breed" features to help Kudu achieve its goals of providing fast analytics on fast data.

At its core, Kudu is a storage engine for tables. It does not provide SQL; there is no SQL rewrite and no SQL access plans as you would see in relational database management systems (RDBMS's). Rather it purely stores structured strongly typed tables and provides efficient methods in which you can access and load data in those tables. Those tables have names and are structured, meaning that they have a defined set of columns, and those columns have data types and column names to go with them.

Kudu stores its own metadata information. Table names, column names, column types, and so on, as well as the data you put in your tables must be stored in the platform. All data, whether it is your own user data or data about your tables (metadata) is just data in the end and needs to be stored. At its very foundation, Kudu stores this data in what's called a *tablet*. Kudu has two different roles to manage these types of data.

Metadata is stored in tablets that are managed by a master server. User data that goes into your tables is stored in tablets that are managed by tablet servers.

Because Kudu stores its own metadata, it doesn't need access to the Hive Metastore. However, if you intend to use Impala on top of Kudu, Impala will need this Hive service.

Both master and tablet servers are similar in that they manage tablets containing physical data that reside on the server on which they are running. A minimum of three servers typically exist for each role, on which data can be both replicated, and, by employing the Raft consensus algorithm, a given server is elected leader for a replica of a tablet.

Figure 2-1 displays a concept for both master and tablet servers that is identical. Although the roles are similar in their concept of data storage, replication, and management, they are different in their purpose and the type of data they store.

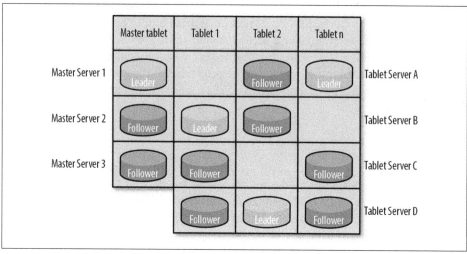

Figure 2-1. Kudu roles

Thus, all the Kudu servers are divided into just two types—the master servers and the tablet servers.

Master Server

The role of the master server is to direct the operations on the Kudu cluster. To define a table or get properties or metadata about a table, clients interact with a single master server. The master server is, in fact, a single-tablet table, storing metadata such as table and column names, column types, and data location, as well as information such as state (whether the table is being created, running, deleting, and more). Essentially, it manages the system "catalog," which is what every RDBMS employs, as well.

The amount of catalog data per table is very small. As such, to improve performance, it keeps a full write-through cache of the entire catalog in memory at all times. The master server is accountable to store the metadata information that will be used by the client application to identify the data location. Even if this role is critical to get access to the data, the master servers don't have a lot of activities to perform. Therefore, you can install them on small hardware. Because the master server will use the configured replication factor to replicate the metadata storage, it is important to have the same number of master servers as the configured replication factor. By default, you should install three servers. This will also ensure the Kudu cluster access high availability.

Even though for production environments multiple master servers are recommended, we will run most of our testing with a single server.

Tablet Server

The tablet server is what we can call a worker node. If we compare it to existing big data technologies, its role can be compared to a mix of an HDFS DataNode and an HBase region server. Its role is to perform all the data-related operations: storage, access, encoding, compression, compaction, and replication. As you can see, compared to the master server, the tablet server is really the service doing all the heavy work. This is where we want to scale. The tablet server is also accountable to replicate the data to the other tablet servers.

- Kudu can work with up to 300 servers. However, to achieve the best stability, at this time, it is recommended to work with fewer than 100 tablet servers.
- A maximum of 2,000 tablets per tablet server, post-replication, is recommended.
- A maximum of 60 tablets per tablet server per table, post-replication, is recommended.
- A maximum 8 TB of data on disk per tablet server is recommended. The total of all the disks on the server can be more than 8 TB and can be shared with HDFS; however, it is recommended to not use more than 8 TB for Kudu data.
- To get the best scan performance on big fact tables, it is recommended to keep a ratio of one tablet for one CPU core. Do not count the replicated tables. You should count only leader tablets. For small dimension tables, a few tablets are fine.

All those numbers are based on Kudu's recommendations at the time of writing. Please refer to the Kudu Apache known issues (*https://kudu.apache.org/docs/ known_issues.html#_scale*) for the latest numbers.

Storage

One of the things that makes Kudu efficient and able to improve both the writes and the reads is the way it stores data. Although many existing big data tools will use specific formats (like HFiles for HBase), Kudu takes the best of all the different applications and formats. If you are already used to the Hadoop ecosystem, many of the storage optimizations listed in the subsections that follow will be familiar to you.

Columnar format.   The first thing to understand is that Kudu will store all of the data in a columnar format. Looking at an example is the best way to understand how this format works and how it can benefit Kudu performance.

Consider a regular file, like a CSV file, in which one line represents a single row, and for which the columns are represented, one after the other, using any kind of format (strings, numbers, etc.) and separated by a given character (see Figure 2-2). Consider that we have 100 rows within our file, and for each row, we have 10 columns, the first one being called id, and another one being called score. Let's consider that we want to calculate the average score for the entire dataset. To perform this operation, we will need to open the file, read the first record, extract the score value, read the second record, extract the score value, and so on until we reach the end of the file. At the end, to perform the required average, you will have read all the columns of all the records. So 100% of the file will need to be loaded from the disk to the system and then parsed.

```
{id;firstname;lastname;login;score;country;duration;ip;date;time}
{4242;Claudio;Viscontino;cvisco;1234;IT;3345;10.10.10.10;2017/11/25;06:12}
{432;Mario;Demers;twit;4;CA;42;10.10.10.10;2016/10/13;23:51}
{3425;Yacil;Powell;actla;1001;US;2592;10.10.10.10;2016/04/30;12:31}
```

Figure 2-2. Flat file CSV format

The concept behind a columnar storage is to regroup the data not by row as in a regular file but, as its name indicates, by column. Therefore, all of the data stored in the first column of all the rows are first stored, then all the second column, and so on. The same way, all the score column content for all the rows is going to be stored in the same section. An application trying to read all the score columns for all the rows will just read the columnar index to figure where the related section is, and then will read only the required data. All the remaining columns and sections will be skipped. If we imagine that all columns are the exact same size, processing an average aggregation on a columnar format file versus a regular one will save about 90% of the disk transfer. Figure 2-3 shows the benefit of this format.

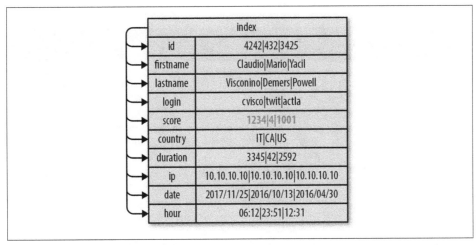

Figure 2-3. Columnar format

As it is easy to determine from Figure 2-3, scanning an entire column becomes very efficient. The downside is that retrieving an entire row will require accessing many blocks to reassemble the row, which obviously isn't efficient.

Thus, the first benefit of a columnar format is low I/O for queries that access a subset of columns. There are additional benefits related to I/O efficiency that we cover now at a high level. Later in the book they are covered in detail.

Now that all values for a given column are stored together, we can exploit this in several ways to reduce the volume of data stored. Imagine a North America–based company's customer table in which one column is the country. Most of the rows will contain Canada, Mexico, or United States. Instead of spreading these values among values of other columns that include other unrelated strings and numbers, they are all grouped together. If we did nothing else, compression (LZ4, Snappy, or zlib) would have significantly more impact than on a row-based format.

However, we can do better. When columnar formats were created and the previous column value locality was created, a new kind of compression was developed called *encoding*. These encodings have the same effect as compression, but with the exception of *plain encoding* transform the data to a smaller representation before generic compression algorithms, which we just discussed, are applied. These encodings are typically data type specific, as shown in Table 2-2.

Table 2-2. Encoding types

Encoding names	Applicable data types	Description
Plain	All	Stores the data in its *natural* format, such as an int32 stored in 4 bytes, and does not reduce data size at all. Useful when CPU is your bottleneck or when the data is precompressed.
Bitshuffle	int8, int16, int32, int64, unixtime_micros, float, and double	Rearranges the bytes before automatically LZ4 compressing. Bitshuffle (*https://github.com/kiyo-masui/bitshuffle*) encoding is a good choice for columns that have many repeated values, or values that change by small amounts when sorted by primary key.
Run Length	Boolean, int8, int16, int32, int64, and unixtime_micros	Stores the count of repeated values and the value itself. As an example, this encoding will allow you to save a lot of space for tables containing application tickets, where 90% of them are in a closed state.
Dictionary	string and binary	Builds a unique list of values and stores an index to the list. In our previous example, we had only three countries, and Canada will be encoded 1, Mexico will be encoded 2, and United States will be encoded 3. Then, for each value, instead of storing a long string, Kudu will store only a number from 1 to 3.
Prefix	string and binary	Common prefixes are compressed in consecutive column values. Multiple good examples are a date field stored as a string where the beginning for the field will almost never change (prefix) whereas the end of the string will almost always change (suffix).

File layout and compactions. One of the biggest challenges of random updates in a storage tool is to expire nonrequired data and keep access to the most recent information—all of that, as fast as possible. To perform this, Kudu implements multiple mechanisms.

Regarding the way Kudu stores data, let's consider two main scenarios. It can be an insertion of new data, or it can be an update of existing data.

At a high level, each write operation will follow these steps:

1. Writes are committed to a tablet's Write Ahead Log (WAL)

2. Inserts are added to the MemRowSet

3. When the MemRowSet is full, it is flushed to disk and becomes the DiskRowSet

Each time Kudu receives new data, it stores that data in memory into what we call a *MemRowSet*. You can view the MemRowSet can be seen as a temporary write buffer. When the MemRowSet is full, it is flush on the disk. Consider Kudu receiving an insert for a table called users to put the value "secret" in the password column for the key "jmspaggi," the last column being empty, and storing that into memory. At flush time, it creates what is called a *DiskRowSet* where it will separate all the columns into different sections, one per column, for that specific row. You can think of a DiskRowSet as a region of a bigger file used to store a specific set of data.

When Kudu later receives another insert for the same table but this time for the row "mkovacev," it first inspects all the existing DiskRowSets as well as the MemRowSet to make sure this row doesn't belong to any of them (see Figure 2-4).

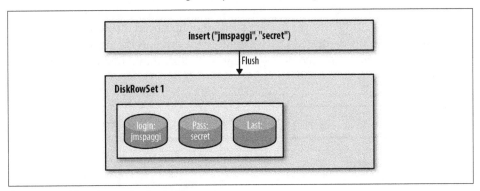

Figure 2-4. First insert in the table

Because none of them contains this row, the row is inserted in the main MemRowSet, which later will be flushed as a new DiskRowSet (Figure 2-5). Kudu needs to perform this validation of the existing DiskRowSets to guarantee uniqueness of the primary key. All data related to a specific primary key is stored, and can be stored, only in a single and same DiskRowSet. If you try to insert a primary key while it already exists, Kudu will return an error, the same as if you try to update a row that doesn't exist.

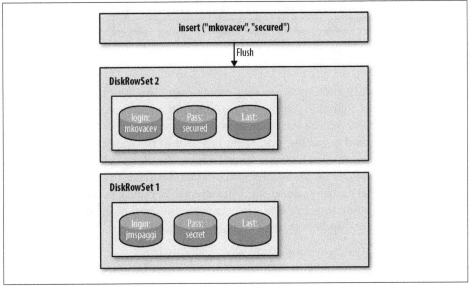

Figure 2-5. Insert in existing table

Now, let's consider an update for the row `jmspaggi` where the `password` field is set to `easy` (Figure 2-6). When Kudu receives the update command, it first determines whether this row is stored in the current MemRowSet or which DiskRowSet already contains the data for it. Using bloom filters to reduce I/Os, it will match the first set containing that row. Now that the correct destination has been identified, the updated column is stored in the dedicated DeltaMemStore for this specific set. Over time, this DeltaMemStore might also become bigger and will flush into a RedoDeltaFile within the DeltaRowSet.

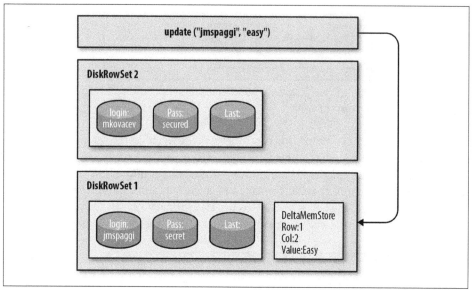

Figure 2-6. Update of existing row

We now have most of the important files represented. The data blocks, called *base data*, one block per column in the table, are stored in a single file. The RedoDelta-Files, one per DeltaMemStore flush, are stored separately. When a client performs a GET operation against a specific row, Kudu has to read the data from the data files and then apply the required updates from reading the RedoDeltaFiles. The more RedoDeltaFiles there are, the slower the read operation will be. To avoid such impact, Kudu performs what we call major delta compactions. To reduce subsequent reads on those files and therefore improve read performances, this operation consists of applying to the data files the updates stored in the RedoDeltaFiles.

Beside major detail compactions, Kudu also performs two other kinds of compactions: delta minor compactions and merging compactions. As the Apache Kudu online documentation describes:

> A *minor* compaction is one that does not include the base data. In this type of compaction, the resulting file is itself a delta file.

and

> A *major* REDO compaction is one that includes the base data along with any number of REDO delta files.

Whereas having to read all RedoDeltaFiles to perform read operations has a cost, merging and rewriting all the data also has one. To ensure the best performance, Kudu will not merge all the RedoDeltaFiles into the existing data files. Indeed, depending on the size of the table, the data file can be big. If there are only a few rows to be updated, rewriting the entire data file to merge those rows will generate a lot of I/Os on the system, and will at the end, only provide a very small improvement on the operations. So while performing compactions, Kudu will generate three sets of data (shown in Figure 2-7):

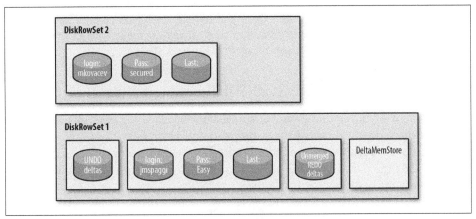

Figure 2-7. Three sets of data are generated while performing compactions

Updated base data

> When a specific column requires a significant amount of updates, Kudu will apply the updates to this data by rewriting it, merged with the updates, into a new dataset.

UNDO deltas

> While applying the delta modifications to the based data, Kudu keeps track of all the updates and stores them into what is called an *undo delta file*. This file is used by Kudu to be able to return a "point in time" value for a past date. By default, Kudu keeps this file for 15 minutes. Therefore, it is possible to query Kudu for what was the exact content of a column up to 15 minutes ago. After 15 minutes, on the next compaction iteration, data older than 15 minutes is expired and the file is removed.

Unmerged REDO deltas

As we have just seen, not all the delta modifications are applied. When modifications are too small to provide benefits to a merge, they are kept on the side for a subsequent compaction. The unmerged redo deltas file contains all the updates not applied to the data files.

Because there is now less data and files to read to rebuild a single row, performance of all subsequent read operations against a compacted Kudu is improved and disk access is reduced.

 When Kudu needs to rewrite data files within a DiskRowSet, it makes sure that rows within the set are rewritten ordered by the key. This allows read requests to not have to read the entire file to find the data they are looking for. Indeed, when looking for a row not present in a file, Kudu can stop parsing the file as soon as the key read from the file is bigger than the requested key.

Kudu Concepts and Mechanisms

The paradigm of distributed systems spreads the load across multiple servers. It allows all the servers to participate in the read and write operations, and therefore improves the throughput and reduces the latency. In this section, we look at how Kudu spreads the data across the servers and how to configure your tables to help Kudu achieve the best possible distribution.

Another very important Kudu concept is the primary key. Kudu regroups and indexes data based on the key. There isn't yet any concept of secondary key or secondary index. Hotspotting (described in the next subsection) usually results from a bad key or partitioning design.

Hotspotting

Before going further, let's describe the most common issue with distributed systems data access. It is called *hotspotting*. We see a hotspot when most read or write (or both) queries are reaching the same server. What we want to achieve is a perfect distribution where all read and write operations are spread across most of the cluster.

Let's look at an example to better understand what hotspotting is. We will use this same example to describe how to correctly design your table. Consider a sensor table in which we store all metrics for a large set of sensors. Data is generated by the sensors, made available and pushed into the cluster, and queried for a specific sensor for its entire lifetime (trend detection, failure detection, etc.). Data is streamed into Kudu, and the information that we have to store is the date, the sensor ID, and its value. Because we want to be able to quickly query the data for a specific day, let's assume that we configure the table to have the date as part of the primary key. (The primary key must be unique. Therefore, it cannot be only the date, unless you are storing only one value per date.) The table is then split into tablets (partitions), each of them storing a range of dates. When data is coming in the system, for the current day, it will reach the tablet server storing the tablet where the range of dates includes today. Because a single key is stored on a single server, no other server in the cluster will store today's related data. Therefore, all the write operations will face a single and unique server. Although this server will probably be overwhelmed, all others will be idle. When the date moves to the end of the range, all operations will move to the next tablet, probably stored in another server, which will, in turn, become hotspotted. This is a very inefficient way to configure a table and design its access pattern. Figure 2-8 illustrates this.

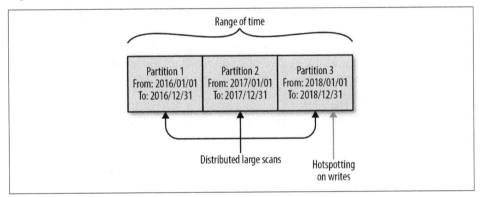

Figure 2-8. Partition by range of time

The opposite issue—the writes are correctly spread across all the servers, but the reads are facing a single server—is very similar.

When thinking about your table, you need to keep in mind three very important things:

- The read access pattern (throughput and latency)
- The write access pattern (throughput and latency)
- Storage overhead (compression ratio)

Partitioning

The way data is retrieved from the cluster, and the way data is coming in, are very important and will drive the table partitioning design, because when developing a use case, the most important thing is the result. Read has been intentionally listed first. Indeed, even if you develop the best possible write partitioning, if your reads don't reply to your use-case requirements (in terms of latency, access pattern, etc.), your project might fail to achieve its final goals.

Storage overhead affects your table when data is spread across the servers. Indeed, as we have seen earlier in the columnar format example, storing similar data together improves the compression. Therefore, depending on your constraints, this might be something to consider.

Kudu can perform two kinds of partitioning (which can be combined): range partitioning and hash partitioning.

Range partitioning

A range partition should be trivial. Refer back to Figure 2-8 to see an example of date range partitioning. We configured the table to have three ranges of dates, with the first tablet storing 2016 data, the second storing 2017 data, and the third storing 2018. As we saw earlier, such partitioning can cause writes to hotspot a server. However, performing a request for a single sensor ID will reach all the tablet servers in parallel and will perform efficiently.

Range partitioning by the sensor ID will provide a nice distribution of the writes. Indeed, for a given day, all inserted data will reach all the servers, each of them containing a subset of the sensors. However, even if all sensors return the same amount of metrics, there might be more sensors within a range versus another one, which will unbalance the partitions and will again affect the performance. Figure 2-9 illustrates this issue.

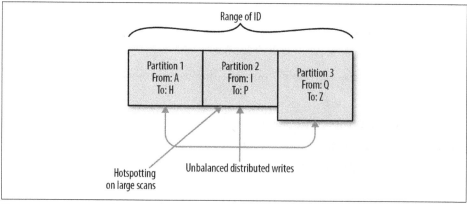

Figure 2-9. Partition by range of ID

Hash partitioning

Using hash partitioning for the sensor ID will help with this challenge. Because all sensors will provide a different hash, the distribution will be even across all the servers and they will all grow at the same pace (Figure 2-10). However, scanning a partition for all the value of a sensor for its lifetime will hotspot the instance and provide poor performance.

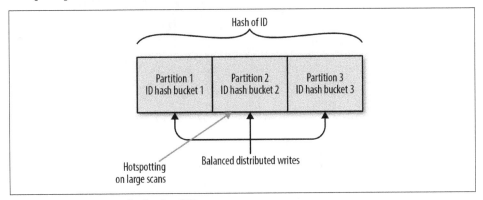

Figure 2-10. Partition by hash of ID

As you can see, hash and range partitions both come with some pros and cons, you need to think them through thoroughly. Combining the two is often the best approach, but, here again, you need to make sure to use the right one for the right dimension. In our given example, we want to spread the writes to multiple tablets and do the same for the reads. We figured that the hash partitioning will give the best result for the sensor ID, whereas the range partitioning will allow us good time-based query access. Combining the two allows us to get good write performances (because hash writes are spread across multiple partitions) and good read performances (because of the buckets, big scans can be run in parallel across multiple servers).

What we call "bucket" here is an ensemble of hashes. As an example, if your sensor ID hashes have values between 00 and 99, one bucket can be all the hashes between 00 and 32, another all the hashes between 33 and 65, and the last hashes between 66 and 99. That way all the sensors will be spread across three buckets. If there is another partitioning dimension, more than one partition can store data for a specific bucket, depending on the other part of the key.

Figure 2-11 illustrates how you should configure this table, using both hash and range partitioning.

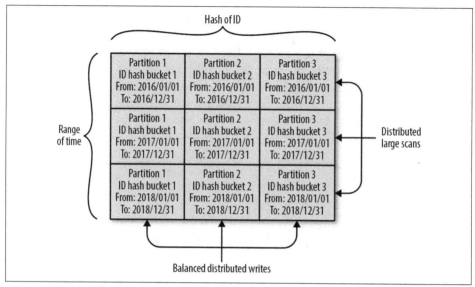

Figure 2-11. Partition by range of time and hash of ID

For more details, refer to Chapter 6.

## CHAPTER 3

Getting Up and Running

The easiest way to get started with any tool is through hands-on experience. The same applies to Kudu. In this chapter, we walk through the various options for installing and configuring Kudu and then introduce you to the basics of an actual installation using RPM packages. Chapter 4 walks you through the different Kudu roles.

Installation

The Apache Kudu website (*http://kudu.apache.org*) is the best place to check or find the latest information on installation options. Currently, there are five main ways to get started developing and using Kudu:

- The Kudu Quickstart Virtual Machine (VM)
- Automated installation using Cloudera Manager on an existing cluster
- Manual installation via packages
- Building from source
- Cloudera Quickstart VM

Apache Kudu Quickstart VM

The Kudu Quickstart VM represents the most accessible and lowest cost way to get started with Kudu (Figure 3-1). The Quickstart VM has the advantage of not requiring a full cluster of machines. In case you break your installation, it also allows you to easily start over from scratch. Using the quickstart VM, we can familiarize ourselves with Kudu's APIs and some of the tools and frameworks that integrate with Kudu, like Impala. The downside, of course, is that because it runs on a VM and not on a cluster of dedicated machines, it's really only relevant for development and demonstration purposes.

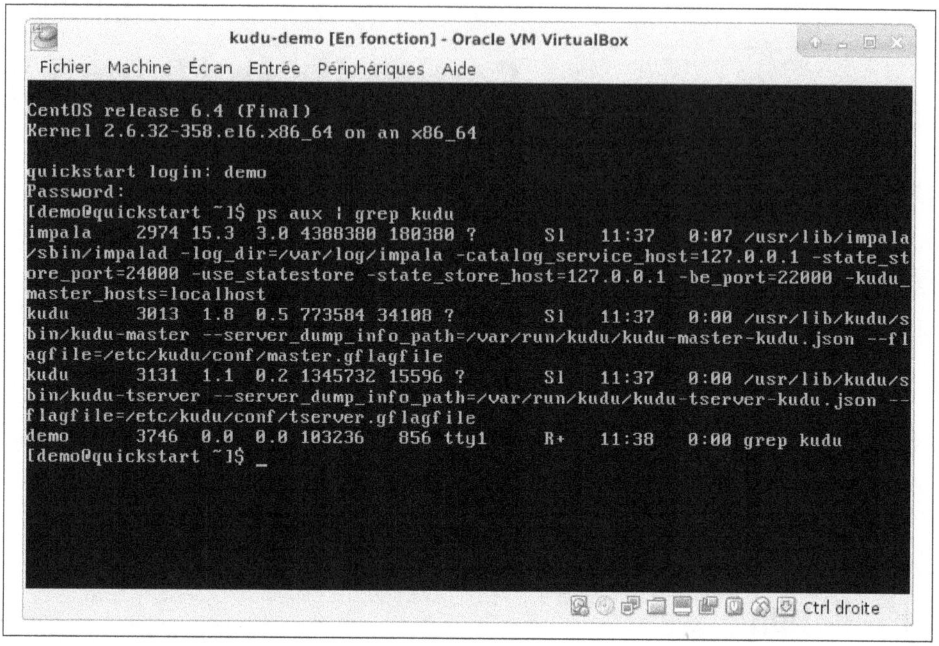

Figure 3-1. Kudu Quickstart VM

Full instructions for using the Quickstart VM are available on the Kudu website. We recommend going to the website for up-to-date instructions. Installing the quickstart comes down to two steps:

1. Download and run Oracle VirtualBox.
2. Download and run the bootstrap script, which will download the Quickstart virtual image and import it into VirtualBox.

From there, you'll have a single-node VM running Kudu and Impala.

When using the VM with the examples in this book, note that the Quickstart doesn't come with all the Hadoop goodies preinstalled. Therefore, if you want to test some of our end-to-end examples that use Spark, SparkStreaming, or Kafka, you'll need to install Spark, Kafka, and Zookeeper manually (Zookeeper because Kafka depends on Zookeeper) or move to a different environment.

Using Cloudera Manager

If you really want to demonstrate the power and scale of Kudu or deploy to production, you'll need to deploy Kudu on a cluster of machines. This is most commonly done using Cloudera Manager and using Cloudera's distribution of Apache Hadoop. Cloudera Manager automates the process of preinstall cluster validation, Kudu cluster installation, configuration, and monitoring.

Rather than using the traditional Linux package manager or Red Hat Package Manager (RPM), most Cloudera users choose to install Kudu using a binary distribution format called parcels. Parcels are a simplified way for Cloudera to package and install the various components of its distribution. Starting from CDH 5.10, Kudu is already included in the parcel and can simply be added to the cluster by using the "Add Service" option.

We recommend using Cloudera Manager and parcels as the easiest way to manage and install Kudu for a production deployment (Figure 3-2). Because the steps for installation might vary slightly with each Cloudera release, consult Cloudera's documentation (*https://www.cloudera.com/documentation.html*).

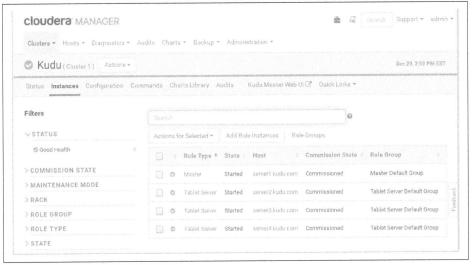

Figure 3-2. Kudu in Cloudera Manager

Cloudera Manager does a good job of configuring Kudu according to best practices but it cannot plan your deployment for you. There are still many other considerations around hardware selection, capacity planning, selecting hosts and roles (master versus tablet servers), and storage locations for Kudu's tablet data and write-ahead logs (WALs). We discuss these in Chapter 4.

Building from Source

If you want to get started with Kudu development or desire the flexibility to have the latest and greatest version of Kudu's upstream code, you can build and install Kudu directly from the source. Check the Apache Kudu website for detailed instructions.

Building from source gives you the chance to get closer to Kudu source code. However, it will require more steps to install, and the issues you might face to build the application might be more difficult to solve. One good side of building from source is that it allows you to easily choose which version of Kudu to test. One downside is integrating it with the other applications of the ecosystem.

Packages

For the purposes of this book, we're going to cover installation using Kudu packages. Packages are available for most major Linux operating systems—like Red Hat, CentOS, SLES, Ubuntu, or Debian Linux. Even though the package-based installation is certainly a little more work than the automated Cloudera Manager installation, you'll see it's fairly simple. In addition, walking through these steps will bring a better understanding of the different components of Kudu. Last, because package installation doesn't require any other application to run (Cloudera Manager, Virtual Box, etc.) it requires fewer resources.

Cloudera Quickstart VM

If what you want to do is try Kudu within the ecosystem, but can't afford to deploy it on a real cluster, a very simple and good alternative is to run it in the Cloudera Quickstart VM (Figure 3-3). Indeed, this VM comes with the entire CDH distribution installed. In addition to Kudu, it also includes Hadoop Distributed File System (HDFS), Impala, Hive, Spark, and so on. You can choose which application you want to run and which one you want to stop. This is a great way to easily play with the integration of the different components. However, because it is a VM and it will run all the services on a single environment, it requires a lot of memory and CPU cycles. The performance will not reflect the performance of a real environment; it takes more time to start and requires more space compared to the Kudu VM. But it will allow you to contain all your tests inside a closed container.

Figure 3-3. Kudu in Cloudera Quickstart VM

This VM comes from different environments. It can run inside VirtualBox, VMWare, KVM, or as a Docker image. You can download the most recent version directly on the Cloudera website (*http://www.cloudera.com/content/support/en/downloads/quick start_vms.html*). After the VM is downloaded, the only thing you need to do is to load it into the environment and start it.

Quick Install: Three Minutes or Less

If your hands are on the keyboard ready to roll, this chapter is for you. The goal? Get Kudu installed and running in three minutes flat. The catch? You have a RHEL/CentOS 7 system already running and you're logged in as a user with sudo access. Here's how to do that:

```
# Set up the repo
$ sudo cat <<EOD >> kudu.repo
[cloudera-kudu]
# Packages for Cloudera's distribution for kudu, Version 5, on RedHat or
# CentOS 7 x86_64
name=Cloudera's Distribution for kudu, Version 5
baseurl=http://archive.cloudera.com/kudu/redhat/7/x86_64/kudu/5/
gpgkey = http://archive.cloudera.com/kudu/redhat/7/x86_64/kudu/ \
    RPM-GPG-KEY-cloudera
gpgcheck = 1
EOD

# Copy the repo file to yum.repos.d
sudo cp kudu.repo /etc/yum.repos.d/

# Install the packages
sudo yum -y install kudu              # Base Kudu files (all nodes)
sudo yum -y install kudu-master       # Kudu master server (master nodes only)
sudo yum -y install kudu-tserver      # Kudu tablet server (tablet nodes only)
sudo yum -y install kudu-client0      # Kudu C++ client shared library
sudo yum -y install kudu-client-devel # Kudu C++ client SDK

# Start up the services
sudo systemctl start kudu-master
sudo systemctl start kudu-tserver
```

If you are running on a Debian-like distribution, keep in mind that Kudu packages are currently available only for Jessie (version 8) and are not yet available for the current Debian stable version (Stretch). You will also need to install the archive key by using the following steps:

```
sudo wget http://archive.cloudera.com/kudu/debian/jessie/amd64/kudu/cloudera.list \
    -O /etc/apt/sources.list.d/cloudera.list
wget https://archive.cloudera.com/kudu/debian/jessie/amd64/kudu/archive.key \
    -O archive.key
sudo apt-key add archive.key
sudo apt-get update

# Install the packages
sudo apt-get install kudu              # Base Kudu files (all nodes)
sudo apt-get install kudu-master       # Kudu master server (master nodes only)
sudo apt-get install kudu-tserver      # Kudu tablet server (tablet nodes only)
sudo apt-get install libkuduclient0     # Kudu C++ client shared library
sudo apt-get install libkuduclient-dev # Kudu C++ client SDK

# Start up the services
sudo systemctl start kudu-master
sudo systemctl start kudu-tserver
```

For now, we do all the preceding steps on a single host. And there you have it, Kudu is up and running (Figure 3-4).

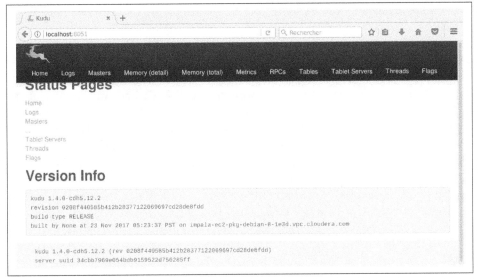

Figure 3-4. Kudu master web user interface

Now point your browser as shown here:

```
Master server: http://<your-host>:8051
Tablet server: http://<your-host>:8050
```

For Kudu itself, that's all there is to it. With these instructions, you can use Kudu as a standalone storage manager for external applications. For example, application servers using Kudu's Java APIs can use Kudu as the persistence layer for time-series applications.

However, because Kudu is part of—but doesn't depend on—the Hadoop ecosystem, most practical use cases require more than just Kudu: for ingesting data, you might want Apache Kafka, StreamSets, or Spark Streaming; for doing machine learning and data processing, you might want Apache Spark; and for interactive SQL, you'll surely want Apache Impala. Practically speaking, Kudu's tight Hadoop ecosystem integrations is one of its strengths; thus, you seldom use it on its own, and you'll probably want to install more than just Kudu.

This leads us to a common question, "What if I want only Kudu and not the rest of Hadoop?" In practice, you'll probably want to have Hadoop, too. Even though Kudu itself has zero dependencies on any other Hadoop component, Kudu is almost always used with Impala, and that's where things become sticky. Impala relies on Hive, and Hive *does* have a dependency on HDFS, meaning that to use Kudu with Impala, you also need Hive and HDFS. There is good news, however, because Kudu and HDFS can easily coexist in harmony and even share disks. You'll want to get the configurations correct, which we discuss in Chapter 4, but for now just know that both storage layers can live together and it's up to you as to whether you use just Kudu or HDFS, as well.

Conclusion

In this chapter, we learned the various ways to install Kudu and walked through an RPM-based installation. As discussed, Kudu's power is enhanced when combined with other Hadoop ecosystem technologies like Spark and Impala. Therefore, to use Kudu's full might, we'd recommend using a Hadoop distribution like Cloudera and a management tool to ease the installation and management, like Cloudera Manager. In future chapters, we delve deeper into how to properly plan and configure your Kudu installation, and then introduce you to the basics of Kudu data management. We use Kudu in conjunction with Apache Impala, a fast, distributed SQL query engine for the Hadoop ecosystem. Then we take a look at how to use Kudu's Java APIs.

## CHAPTER 4

Kudu Administration

The administrator's dream is to work with a system that is resilient, fault tolerant, simple to scale, monitor, and adapt as requirements change. Even better is a system that is self-healing, shows warning signs early, and lets the administrator go to sleep knowing that the system will run in a *predictable* way.

Kudu is designed and built from the ground up to be fault tolerant, scalable, and resilient and provides administrators with the means to see what's happening in the system, both through available APIs and visually through a web user interface (UI) and a handy command-line interface (CLI).

In this chapter, we get you started as an administrator so that you can hit the ground running. Installation options are covered in previous chapters, so we begin here by looking at planning for your Kudu deployment and then walk through some of the most common and useful administrator tasks.

Planning for Kudu

Let's begin by taking time to understand how to appropriately plan for a Kudu deployment.

 Kudu is fully open source and made available with documentation, downloads, overviews, and more provided at *http:// kudu.apache.org/*. However, Kudu might also be included in various Hadoop distributions. If going with a distribution, always refer to the documentation provided by the vendor as deployment strategies may vary.

Kudu can be installed as its very own cluster with no dependency on any other components; however, we expect that many installations will be on existing Hadoop clusters. Knowing how to plan, size, and place Kudu services in relation to all your other Hadoop components is also be covered.

Master and Tablet Servers

Before we jump into hardware planning and where we will place the Kudu services, as an administrator we need to understand the primary two components we need to think about in Kudu: the master and tablet servers. These servers manage tables, or rather, *tablets*, that make up the contents of a table. Tablets are then replicated, which is why they are also known as replicas.

Typically, you start a cluster with three master servers. Consensus needs to be reached between these master servers so that they agree among themselves which server is the leader. This decision-making process must have a majority of servers "vote" to make the final decision (e.g., 2 of the 3, or 3 of the 5, and so on), and the decision they make is final. This procedure is both fault tolerant and performant, using what's called the Raft consensus algorithm (*https://raft.github.io/*), which is a variation of the well-known Paxos consensus algorithm. Three or five master servers are good examples of the number of master servers to plan for, whereas seven master servers would be considered excessive. The number *must* be odd, where you can lose up to $(n - 1) / 2$ servers and still be able to make progress. In the event that *more* than $(n - 1) / 2$ servers fail, the master service will no longer be making progress and thus is no longer available to the cluster.

Tables break down their data into partitions stored in this concept of "tablets," which are then replicated where the default replication factor is 3. Hence, each tablet is often referred to as a *replica* that contains a portion of data that makes up a table.

Master servers maintain metadata or catalog information about all the tables users create. A single system catalog table is created to handle metadata for various objects created in Kudu. This table is designed to have exactly one partition, and therefore, one tablet.

This metadata is currently stored in a table that resides on the master servers, which has exactly one tablet stored on the master servers.

Let's say you decide to create table T, which we depict with the logical box illustrated in Figure 4-1. Data for this table is broken down into chunks called tablets, which we show as having three tablets: Tablet 1, Tablet 2, and Tablet 3. Table T also stores your inserted data.

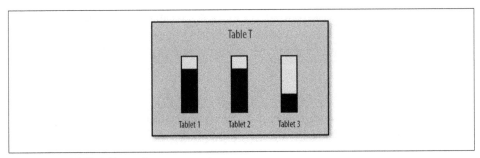

Figure 4-1. Table T logical representation

This representation of the table, broken down into tablets, is spread further across nodes by having each of these tablets replicated across several tablet servers. In this example of three tablet servers (Figure 4-2), we mark each tablet as 1, 2, 3, but because there are multiple replicas, one of these replicas is the leader (denoted by L) whereas the other two are followers (denoted by F).

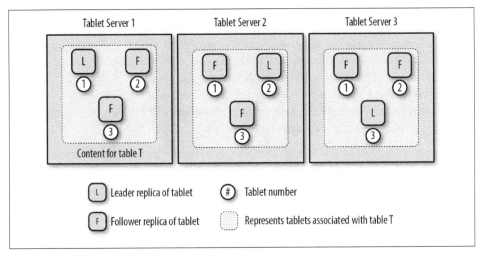

Figure 4-2. Table T replicated

Raft consensus is used to elect a leader among the tablet replicas on the tablet servers.

Master tablets, because they contain only metadata, really should not be as hot as your user tablets given that we could expect that you're not performing Data Definition Language (DDL) operations as fast as you are loading your data into tablets. Likewise, these tables should never grow as large as your user tables, so the requirements for the master servers for storage, memory, and CPU will be a lot more modest than your tablet servers themselves.

The system catalog table is defined as a three column table consisting of entry_type, entry_id, and metadata. The catalog manager loads this table into memory and constructs three hashmaps to allow fast lookups of the catalog information. The catalog information is compact, and since it contains only metadata and no real user data, it will remain small and not require large amounts of resources such as memory and CPU.

 Master servers contain only metadata about your user tables. Therefore, storage, memory, and compute resource requirements are considerably smaller than tablet servers. Sizing details are discussed later in the chapter.

To provide a visual aid, Figure 4-3 shows some of the high-level concepts that we have just covered. In this example, three master servers exist and each manages a single tablet for the system catalog table that master servers maintain (metadata). Of these tablets, one will be elected the leader, whereas the others are followers providing high availability for this data. Finally, we have a write-ahead log existing on each of the master servers.

On the lower half of the diagram, we have tablet servers that manage the tables you create in Kudu. We have N tablet servers, and we depict tables with the dotted line. Table data is stored in tablets that are spread across the various tablet servers. Once again we see one tablet is selected to be the leader, denoted by L, while the followers, denoted by F, for a given tablet replica are found on other tablet servers. We also show that for each Kudu table, a separate write-ahead log (shown in Figure 4-3 as "WAL") is created and exists on each tablet server.

In fact, master servers and tablet servers are identical at this high-level view, showing the idea that the same concepts exist across both of these servers.

How many tablet servers should you plan for? Of course, the answer is going to be *it depends*. Kudu stores data in columnar, Parquet-like format, using various encodings and compression strategies. Because it is *Parquet-like*, from a storage *capacity* perspective, you can roughly examine how much capacity your data occupies in Parquet format files in your HDFS filesystem (or otherwise) and use that as a rough measuring stick for how your data would look stored in Kudu.

Traditional Hadoop-related technologies were not built from the ground up to effectively use solid-state drives (SSDs) because SSDs were too expensive. Kudu being a modern platform, takes advantage of SSD performance, and can make use of NVM Express (NVMe), extremely fast PCIe-attached flash adapters. SSD drives are still not quite as dense as hard-disk drives (HDDs) today and this means that typically these hardware configurations would have less overall storage density per node than HDD configurations.

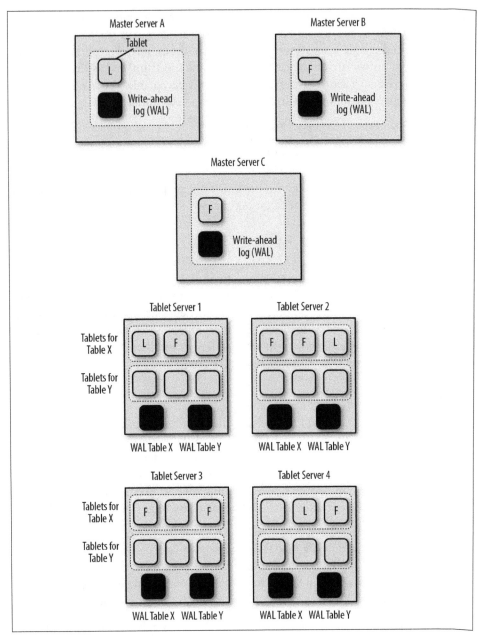

Figure 4-3. High-level architecture

That being said, as it stands today, a reasonable *default* configuration would plan for a range of less than 10 TB of data on disk for a given tablet server (includes storage of all tablet replicas) and a maximum range of low thousands of replicas per tablet server. These numbers are on the cautious end of the spectrum, and as Kudu matures, more data stored on a tablet server will be perfectly acceptable. From a tablet server count perspective, the following formula might help your initial sizing:

```
d = 120 TB : Size of dataset in parquet format
k =   8 TB : Target max disk capacity per tablet server
p =     25% : Percentage overhead to leave
r =      3 : Tablet replication factor
```

Now from a capacity view, we can do the following simple calculation, to determine the number of tablet servers we need for our dataset:

```
t = (d / (k * (1 - p))) * r
t = (120 / (8 * (1 - 0.25))) * 3
t = 20 tablet servers
```

There are more considerations to take into account, such as planning for how many replicas would exist on a tablet server to ensure that we are within the low thousands range. Those calculations depend on partitioning schema strategy as well as the number of tables expected to be defined in your environment. We leave it to you to review Chapter 6, which specifically goes into schema design, and then it's a matter of simple math to ensure that you meet these best-practice ranges.

Write-Ahead Log

For every modification made to a table, and thereby a tablet and replicas, an entry is made in the tablet's write-ahead log (WAL). There is an entire suite of parameters controlling different aspects of log segments that are written to the WAL. Segments have size and properties related to preallocated storage, perhaps asynchronously. They have a compression codec as well as minimum and maximum number of segments that should be kept around so that other peers might be able to catch up if they've fallen behind.

The WAL is an append-only log that at first glance would look like the disk just needs to be able to perform high sequential writes. Even though these are append-only logs, there are logs for each tablet on the master or tablet server. If multiple tables are being written to, from the disk's point of view, it is very much a random write pattern.

If we look at performance characteristics of HDDs versus SSDs from a random write workload perspective where we're interested in a high amount of low-latency I/O operations (as opposed to high throughout sequential write operations), SSDs have an enormous advantage. Where HDDs will have I/O operations per second (IOPS) on the order of the low hundreds, SSDs will have IOPS in the thousands to tens of thousands of operations. In 2016, Samsung showcased a million IOPS SSD, which is

certainly orders of magnitude faster than HDDs! Just looking at write IOPS alone, it is in the low hundreds of thousands of IOPS; needless to say, these are drastic differences. Read/write latency is below 100 microseconds, whereas HDD is in the 10 millisecond range. You get the idea.

Given the type of workload, it is best to plan on a fast SSD NVMe solution for the WAL.

Capacity-wise, default log segment sizes are 8 MB with a minimum of 1 log segment kept and a maximum of 80. This is not a hard maximum, because there are some cases in which a leader tablet might continue to accept writes while the replicas on other peers are restarting or are down.

Kudu might improve the disk usage of the WAL with various techniques in future releases, though we can still plan around these worst-case scenarios. If all tablets are writing at the same time, and staying within the current recommended range of the low thousands, say, 2,000 tablets per tablet server, the math is simple:

```
8 MB/segment * 80 max segments * 2000 tablets = 1,280,000 MB = ~1.3 TB
```

Scalability and density improvements are continually being made, and the preceding calculation is truly in the absolute worst-case scenario. So provisioning your very fast storage for around this mark of 1.3 TB is more than reasonable.

Typical 2U servers used as worker nodes in a big data environment will have 2× SSD in the back of the unit for the operating system (OS), and either 12 x 3.5″ LFF or 24 x 2.5″ SFF drive bays in the front. There are a few options for how to prepare storage for the WAL:

- Install dedicated SSDs in a drive bay on the front
- Make one of the two SSDs in the back dedicated to the WAL (losing out on Redundant Array of Independent Disks [RAID] protections for the OS)
- Create a physical or logical partition on the pair of rear SSDs, and dedicate a mount point to the Kudu WAL
- Install an NVMe PCIe SSD interface–based flash drive

For large production deployments, we do not recommend setting the WAL to a dedicated HDD, or worse a shared HDD with other services, because it will affect both write performance and recovery times in failure scenarios.

Performance of the various storage options vary incredibly. Table 4-1 summarizes them for your consideration.

Table 4-1. HDD versus SSD versus NVMe PCIe flash storage

Storage medium	IOPS	Throughput (MB/sec)
HDD	55-180	50-180
SSD	3,000-40,000	300-2000 (SAS max is 2,812 MB/sec)
NVMe PCIe flash storage	150,000 up to 1 million+	Up to 6,400 (6.4 GB/sec)

Some of the ranges are extremely large as there are a number of factors at play such as block sizes, read workloads versus write workloads, and more. However, the message is clear that PCI attached storage can yield an overwhelming increase in both IOPS and throughput, which greatly benefits Kudu workloads.

Data Servers and Storage

When it comes to your data—what we call user data—this is where it becomes simple. Provide as many available HDDs (or better yet SSDs!) on your server as possible for storage. You can scale out your servers, at will, though note that data is not, as of yet, automatically distributed across new servers added to the cluster.

It is highly likely that you will want to enable Kudu in an HDFS-backed big data cluster. You can configure Kudu storage directories on the very same HDFS-specific mount points. For example, if you have a disk that is partitioned and formatted with a filesystem, mounted on /disk1 you might likely have a directory called /disk1/dfs representing the DataNode of your distributed filesystem, HDFS, installation. Go ahead and create a directory called /disk1/tserver for your Kudu content.

Some consider whether to dedicate a few disks on a server just for Kudu and then others for HDFS. Although this is possible and can even in fact yield a performance improvement, it is not advisable to go through the trouble of overhead in management, dealing with expansion and checking which disks are really being used effectively.

HDFS is certainly aware of how much capacity is still available per disk, and in 2016, it even introduced the ability to rebalance data blocks within a DataNode (HDFS-1312: Re-balance disks within a DataNode) (*https://issues.apache.org/jira/browse/HDFS-1312*) according to either round-robin or available space policies to ensure usage is even.

> At the time of this writing, it is recommended to not store more than 8 TB of Kudu data per tablet server. This is after considering replication as well as compression in well-packed columnar storage formats. Density per node is sure to improve as the product continues to gain adoption and maturity, though it is currently an important point to consider, especially with regard to worrying about sharing disks with other services such as HDFS.

Aside from replica data (i.e., user data), the WAL tablet servers have metadata that they store, as well. The directories where this metadata is written are configurable, and it is important that you place them on the highest performing drive with high throughput and low latency, such as an SSD. In previous releases to v1.7, this metadata is written to the first entry listing the set of data directories on a tablet server. From v1.7 and onward, the default directory is now the directory specified by the WAL directory. However, there is a new parameter, `--fs_metadata_dir`, that allows you to take control and specify where the metadata should be placed.

Placing the metadata on the WAL or nondata disk is helpful because this data can grow over time, and your data drives can become skewed in how they are populated.

Replication Strategies

As you define your replication factor for a given table, tablet servers will strive to ensure that that replication factor is preserved for all the tablets within that table.

Hence, if a tablet server goes down, the number of replicas might have dropped from three replicas to two, Kudu will look to heal these tablets quickly.

The replication strategy primarily is use is named 3-4-3, which is intended to say that if a tablet server goes down, before evicting that failed replica, Kudu will first add a replacement replica and then decide it is time to evict the failed one.

Another strategy, named 3-2-3, would evict that failed replica immediately and then proceed to add a new one. However, for systems that might go offline only periodically and come back up, it causes a much longer delay in becoming part of the cluster again.

In environments that might have more frequent server failures, this becomes important for overall stability. Otherwise you would have a situation in which the failed tablet server has all its tablets evicted immediately, leading to a lot of work to bring it back into play. This actually allows for very fast recovery when a tablet server goes down only briefly and then returns.

There are situations in which Kudu will perform the 3-2-3 mechanism, but only if the failure that one of the tablet servers experiences is known to be unrecoverable. Otherwise, a new tablet replica will be created on a new host, and if the failed tablet server happens to come back to life, no harm done, and the new copy being created is simply canceled.

Deployment Considerations: New or Existing Clusters?

There are three different general scenarios in which you might configure Kudu:

- A brand-new Kudu-only cluster
- A brand-new Hadoop cluster that inclues Kudu
- An existing Hadoop cluster to which we add Kudu

We cover considerations for each of these scenarios.

New Kudu-Only Cluster

When embarking on creating a brand-new cluster targeted for Kudu workloads, in an ideal world, servers would be ordered with all data drives being SSDs, plus an NVMe PCIe SSD interface–based flash drive for the WAL.

Actually, this is not far-fetched for a Kudu-only cluster. Considering that the overall recommended storage density for Kudu today should be on the order of approximately 10 TB, it is easy to accommodate a purchase of a typical 1U server, with two SSDs in the back for the OS and eight SSDs for data coming in around the 1.8 TB mark, which would yield 14.4 TB of raw capacity per server. Add to that a 1 TB NVMe PCIe attached flash drive, and you have a very capable cluster meeting the design goals of Kudu (Figure 4-4).

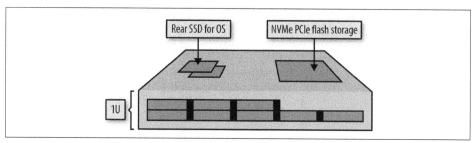

Figure 4-4. Kudu-only cluster server example

New Hadoop Cluster with Kudu

Although Kudu can very much be a standalone cluster, it is more common and expected for it to be part of a larger Hadoop ecosystem that would include HDFS, along with the various other processing services on top, such as Hive, Impala, HBase, YARN, Solr, and Spark.

In this case, Kudu integrates right into the rest of the ecosystem seamlessly, and for write-heavy workloads in particular, we want to ensure the placement of the WAL is on the fastest medium we could include.

We propose two different approaches for planning in this kind of environment: one in which the WAL would be on NVMe PCIe–attached flash storage, and the second using one of the data drives dedicated to the WAL.

Starting with the three master servers in a typical Kudu deployment, this fits in nicely with the master servers used in a common Hadoop environment.

Typically in Hadoop, we will have nodes with "master" type services, such as the following:

- Active/Standby NameNode for HDFS High Availability, where the JournalNodes are spread across three master servers leveraging dedicated spindles
- ZooKeeper instances spread across three master servers, provided with dedicated spindles
- YARN Active/Standby ResourceManager plus the YARN Job History Server
- One or more HiveServer2 instances (though these can be on edge nodes, as well)
- One or more HBase master servers
- Spark Job History Server
- Impala StateStore and CatalogStore
- Sentry Active/Standby nodes
- Multiple Oozie Services

Depending on which distribution of Hadoop you are running and which services you have deployed, there might be other services that are spread across these three master servers.

Hence, it is a natural fit for Kudu to require a fast drive for the WAL even here, similar to JournalNodes and ZooKeeper with their dedicated drives. We want Kudu to have its own fast drive, as well.

Again, we reuse the idea of using a typical 1U server with eight drives out front, and suggest that all of these be SSD drives. We rely on a NVMe PCIe flash storage adapter for the Kudu master WAL, and accommodate dedicated drives (a pair of drives in RAID1) for various services like the NameNode, JournalNode, and ZooKeeper services (Figure 4-5).

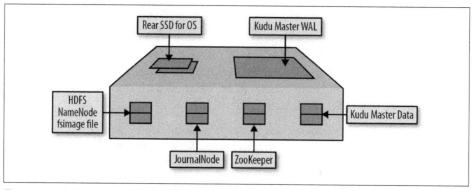

Figure 4-5. Master server for Hadoop with Kudu

The second option we offer here is to consider using a typical 2U server that has two SSDs in the back for the OS and twelve 3.5″ drives in the front. With each pair of drives in RAID1 configuration, we end up with six block devices made available to the OS. A filesystem is then formatted and mounted on each of these block devices, where we lay out each filesystem to be dedicated to the following:

- NameNode fsimage files
- Hive Metastore database (typically MySQL or Postgres)
- HDFS JournalNode
- ZooKeeper logs
- Kudu master data
- Kudu master WAL

Only the last four drives for Kudu would be optimized with SSDs, but the rest of the services would benefit from SSDs as well. In this example, we do not configure a NVMe PCIe–attached flash storage device in an attempt to fully utilize the drive bays available in 2U units while still providing more than enough capability for Kudu (Figure 4-6).

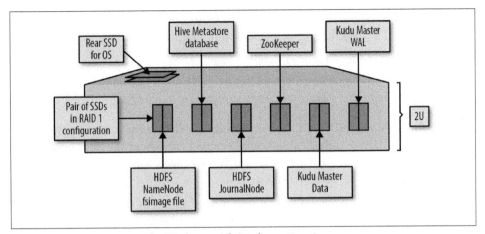

Figure 4-6. Master server for Hadoop with Kudu, option 2

The next consideration is planning for the Kudu tablet servers amidst the Hadoop ecosystem, namely Kudu data on each of the HDFS DataNodes. These are the scale-out servers that are used for a variety of other services in the Hadoop ecosystem, and we refer to them as *worker nodes* as a more generic term.

Worker nodes are most often represented in the Hadoop space as 2U, industry-standard servers with either twelve 3.5″ drive bays in the front or twenty-four 2.5″ drive bays in the front for data. There are typically two 2.5″ drive bays in the rear of these units meant for the OS.

The ideal strategy is to have NVMe PCIe–attached flash storage in the 2U servers specific to the WAL for the Kudu tablet servers. Flash storage would be dedicated to the WAL and would maximize write performance to Kudu. Next, the data drives in these units would ideally be all SSDs to benefit Kudu. However, it is understandable and still expected that perhaps even for newly provisioned environments, HDDs would still be commonplace. They still provide much more density per server, which may be an important requirement, especially for data sitting in HDFS.

As soon as users learn that Kudu sits completely outside of HDFS and the rest of the Hadoop ecosystem, the common thinking is to start isolating drives for Kudu versus HDFS. Although this is possible and certainly does isolate workloads from a storage perspective, it can end up being too restrictive in the long run. There might be workloads today that require more HDFS capacity; however, in the future, perhaps more of those workloads will move to Kudu. Making changes in storage configurations after the fail could prove to be very costly and cumbersome.

We would suggest that you use the same disks assigned for HDFS data for Kudu data as well, except for the actual directory path given to each service.

For example, let's assume that /disk1 is an ext4 filesystem that sits on top of a single JBOD disk. For HDFS, normally, you would define a path under this directory such as:

```
/disk1/dfs : Directory for HDFS data
```

For Kudu, we simply would add a new directory such as the following:

```
/disk1/tserver : Directory for Kudu data
```

Hence, both Kudu and HDFS sit in their own directories on the same filesystem and device volume. HDFS and Kudu alike would simply know about the total capacity left on a given drive, and an HDFS rebalance might take place, for example, if Kudu data is hotspotting much of its data on this one node.

The one situation for which we would recommend different disks is in the case of encryption at rest. You should configure HDFS with HDFS Transparent Encryption, while Kudu, at the moment, relies on full-disk encryption techniques at the device level in order to have data encrypted at rest.

If you select servers with all SSD drives, both HDFS and Kudu would benefit. If all the drives are HDD, HDFS and Kudu would use them, though Kudu would likely be a little more affected in its ability to read/write. Still, this is expected and commonplace, and many workloads already run with this behavior so it should not be considered a deterrent.

The 3.5″ HDD drives today can easily be in the range of 6 to 8 TB in capacity, and reserving one or a pair of these for the Kudu WAL would result in a lot of wasted capacity given to the WAL instead of to data. Thus, we certainly suggest NVMe PCIe–attached flash storage. This kind of approach would yield the hardware topology as shown in Figure 4-7.

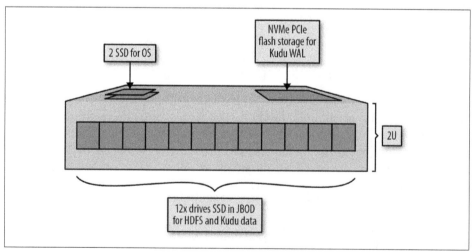

Figure 4-7. Tablet server for Hadoop with Kudu, option 1

Another consideration is a topology without using NVMe PCIe–attached storage. In this case, to ensure we don't waste as much space for the WAL, we take a 2U server with twenty-four 2.5″ drive bays. We take just a single drive bay to dedicate to the Kudu WAL, and ideally, we could make this one drive SSD (if the rest of them aren't already).

This is better depicted by Figure 4-8.

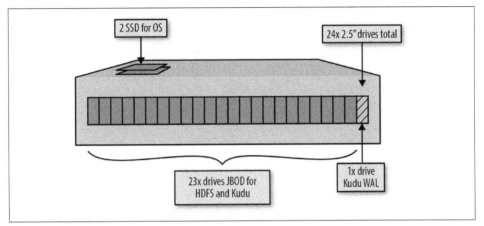

Figure 4-8. Tablet server for Hadoop with Kudu, option 2

With this strategy, if you ever remove Kudu from this cluster, that disk drive dedicated to the WAL can quickly be repurposed for HDFS, for example. So it gives some flexibility as well.

Add Kudu to Existing Hadoop Cluster

The previous section went through a discussion about optimal configuration of Kudu in a brand-new Hadoop environment. Our goal, obviously, is to get as close as possible to those topologies.

The quickest way to get to an optimal Kudu configuration is to order and install a new NVMe PCIe flash storage device. By doing so, you get closer to the configuration as depicted in an earlier diagram, shown in Figure 4-9.

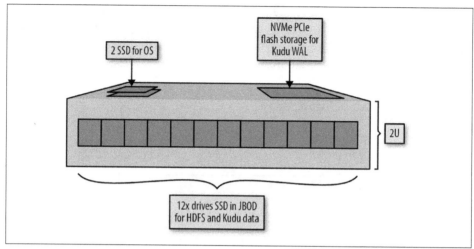

Figure 4-9. Adding NVMe PCIe flash storage for WAL

The new NVMe PCIe flash storage device is used for the WAL exclusively. Meanwhile, the Kudu data directories on the Kudu tablet servers would share the same filesystem mount points assigned to HDFS. Hence, consider the following filesystem mount points:

```
/data1
/data2
...
/data12
```

The path to HDFS would likely be something like:

```
/data1/dfs
...
/data12/dfs
```

We would essentially simply add Kudu directories as follows:

```
/data1/tserver
...
/data12/tserver
```

This allows for clean separation between Kudu and HDFS in terms of directories managed by each service, while at the same time maximizing the utilization of the disk itself.

In Figure 4-10, we show how disk space might be occupied by the various services. To the OS, and even to the services themselves, they can detect simply how much space is left on the disk itself. Balancing and disk selection will automatically try to keep the disks approximately evenly utilized so that, at the end of the day, the disks will naturally be used up more and more evenly.

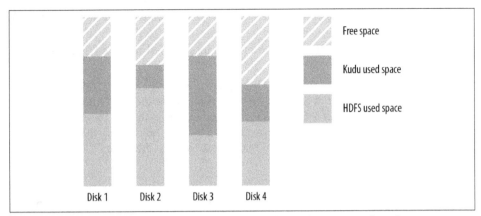

Figure 4-10. Recommended—use the same drives for both HDFS and Kudu

In general, we do not want to start disabling HDFS from using certain drives just so Kudu can have its own dedicated devices. If we did so, then the filesystem layout would look like this example:

```
/data1/dfs
...
/data6/dfs
/data7/tserver
...
/data12/tserver
```

This makes it very difficult to adjust requirements in the future, at which point we might end up having some disks that are extremely full for a given service, whereas the others might not be. Achieving a good balance is very difficult in this scenario. Figure 4-11 illustrates how that might end up looking.

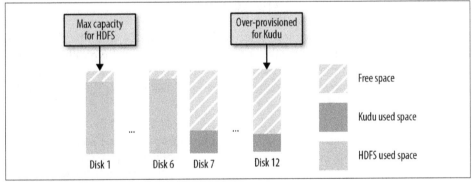

Figure 4-11. Discouraged—segregate HDFS and Kudu drives

If adding an NVMe–PCIe attached flash storage device for the WAL is not possible, it is at this point that we can consider putting the WAL on one of the existing data drives. However, in this case, we want to make sure that we use that drive exclusively for the WAL in Kudu; hence, it would be recommended to first remove that device from being used by HDFS. The transition would look something like Figure 4-12.

 Remember that disks in Hadoop are used not only by HDFS, but are also used as scratch directories for services such as YARN and Impala. If this is the case in your environment, you want to remove the usage of this disk drive from all existing services, so that the disk is fresh and dedicated to the Kudu WAL on the server.

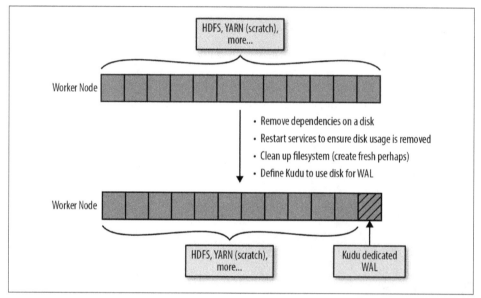

Figure 4-12. Transition worker node to also be tablet server

Of course, this retrofit is a little more painful when it is a DataNode and only 12 disks exist on the server. You lose capacity on every worker node, and typically, the WAL should not require the full capacity of the entire disk. In environments with 24 disks per worker node, it is likely much easier to give up a disk because they are typically smaller-capacity drives.

 Often, people attempt to add Kudu to a subset of worker nodes in an existing environment. Although technically doable, remember the caveats with this include a possible lopsided configuration between the worker nodes (some will have the 23 drives for HDFS/Kudu data + 1 for Kudu WAL, others will have 24 drives for HDFS), as well as encouraging more remote reads from Impala and Spark when processing from Kudu. Hence, this is generally discouraged.

Remember that a lot of the recommendations listed here are meant for peak-performance production clusters. In development environments, certainly get your feet wet and try out the functionality of Kudu by doubling up disk responsibilities such as putting the WAL and data directories on the same disks.

Web UI of Tablet and Master Servers

Visually being able to quickly see how your Kudu deployment is configured, what tables exist, and where tablets reside is crucial to being an effective administrator.

Kudu ships with a web UI, which is the first place to assess these points.

Master Server UI and Tablet Server UI

The master server UI and tablet server Web UI have a common look and feel. Some of the commonalities include the capability to view the following:

Logs
> Last snippet of the log shown in the UI, and it shows a clear path to where you can find the logs on the server.

Memory
> Segregated into detailed memory breakdowns as well as summary totals to get a good understanding of where memory is being used.

Metrics
> An API endpoint intended to provide many metrics in JSON format, easily consumable by JSON parsers, to get at the metrics you like.

Remote procedure calls (RPCs)
> Listing of actively running and sampled remote procedure calls in JSON format.

Threads
> A view into threads, the amount of CPU they consume along with cumulative I/O-wait measurements. Threads are categorized into thread groups, which make it easy to drill down.

Flags
> All of the flags defined at server startup time. This is a good way to validate whether your changes are taking effect as well as seeing the default settings at a glance.

Of course, master and tablet servers have different roles. Hence these UI elements are specific to the type of server you're analyzing.

Master Server UI

The master server UI has the following unique properties:

Masters
> See the currently elected leader as well as the list of masters in your environment.

Tables
> A list of all the tables.

Tablet servers
> List of all the registered Tablet servers, their universal identifier, or UUID, along with RPC and HTTP address information and more.

Tablet Server UI

The tablet server UI has the following unique properties:

Dashboards
> Provides a view into currently running scans, transactions, and maintenance operations being performed on the tablet server.

Tablets
> List of tablets (replicas) being managed by this server.

The Kudu Command-Line Interface

Visuals are important for administrators to get a quick and easy overview of their environment. However, administrators often find themselves interested in a common set of detailed information and metrics as they zero in on what is most important to them. Thus, it makes a lot of sense for administrators to become familiar with the command-line interface (CLI) provided by Kudu. We summarize here some of the key operations that you can perform using the CLI in order to get to know your cluster well, understand the state that it is in, and make the right decisions when it comes to maintenance and other operations.

The CLI is accessed starting with the kudu executable followed by a command that determines what group of operations you'd like to perform. Commands are broken down into operations on the *cluster*, the *filesystem*, *local* and *remote* replicas, *metadata file* operations, *master and tablet server* operations, and table and WAL operations, while along the way checking on the health and integrity of the data itself.

Let's go through each group to see a few examples of what information you can obtain and monitor. We leave it to you to dig into the details of the commands in the Kudu documentation given that they are bound to change and evolve over time.

Cluster

At the cluster level, the only real command at your disposal is to perform a health check:

```
kudu cluster ksck <comma-separate-master-server-addresses>
```

The `comma-separate-master-server-addresses` might look as follows:

```
master-server1,master-server2
```

 Note that we don't specify the port number here. If you're using the default port that Kudu ships with, you typically should not need to specify the port number for these types of commands. If you change the port the master servers operate on, you will need to specify the port numbers in these commands.

Information returns the health state of all the tables and gathers information from all the tablet servers the masters know about. In particular, it provides information such as the following:

- Cluster health
- Data integrity
- Under-replicated tablets
- Unreachable tablet servers
- Tablets with no leader

You might want to perform checksums on your table data to ensure that the data written to disk is as expected. You can do so by using the following simple command:

```
kudu cluster ksck ip-172-31-48-12,ip-172-31-59-149   -checksum_scan
-tables=python-example
```

Performing checksum on your table is good practice especially after performing maintenance work or if there was an unexpected system outage in your data center. It helps to validate that your tables and the data within them did not become corrupted. More options are available to limit scans to specific tablet servers, improve concurrency of the checksums, and more.

Snapshot checksums, which are on by default, take a snapshot of the data as it exists when you have run this command. This is particularly helpful for highly volatile tables and allows these tasks to be performed in parallel.

Filesystem

This tool provides Kudu filesystem checks, formatting, and more. Kudu's notion of the "filesystem" is really a virtual concept that sits on top of your operating system's filesystem (such as ext4, xfs, etc) defined on the disks themselves. Exploring, formatting and checking the filesystem can be useful to have a better understanding of Kudu itself.

> The file *.gflagfile* contains the Kudu service startup options, which can sometimes be helpful to dig into how the Kudu processes were actually started. This is especially true if you set certain parameters but they do not seem to actually have any effect. In this file you can see whether your parameter was actually set as a startup flag.

check

Checking the filesystem for errors needs to be run as root. You must supply the *WAL* directory and then can provide a comma-separated list of data directories. An easy way to check what those directories are is to check the *.gflagfile* in use for your server.

You can find the *.gflagfile* by running the ps command:

```
ps -ef | grep kudu

# See output such as the following
kudu      10148     1  0 Aug15 ?        00:04:32
/usr/lib/kudu/sbin/kudu-tserver
--server_dump_info_path=/var/run/kudu/kudu-tserver-kudu.json
--flagfile=/etc/kudu/conf/tserver.gflagfile
```

Notice the flagfile option:

```
--flagfile=/etc/kudu/conf/tserver.gflagfile
```

Now grep for the fs parameters in that file:

```
grep "fs_" /etc/kudu/conf/tserver.gflagfile

# See output such as the following
--fs_wal_dir=/var/lib/kudu/tserver
--fs_data_dirs=/var/lib/kudu/tserver
```

What we see here is that these directories are the same for the WAL and data directories. Kudu comes with filesystem "check" tools, which will provide a full block manager report that shows whether the Kudu filesystem is healthy. Things like missing blocks or orphaned blocks are warning signs that maybe something is not quite right with this filesystem.

When we do the fs check on the WAL directory, it (in this case) automatically finds the data directory as well as performs the checking for you:

```
sudo kudu fs check -fs_wal_dir=/var/lib/kudu/tserver/wals
```

The preceding output will then look something like this:

```
uuid: "e60fc0618b824f6a994748c053f9f4c2"
format_stamp: "Formatted at 2017-08-16 04:36:00 on ip-172-31-59-149.ec2.internal"
Block manager report
--------------------
1 data directories: /var/lib/kudu/tserver/data
Total live blocks: 0
Total live bytes: 0
Total live bytes (after alignment): 0
Total number of LBM containers: 0 (0 full)
Total missing blocks: 0
Total orphaned blocks: 0 (0 repaired)
Total orphaned block bytes: 0 (0 repaired)
Total full LBM containers with extra space: 0 (0 repaired)
Total full LBM container extra space in bytes: 0 (0 repaired)
Total incomplete LBM containers: 0 (0 repaired)
Total LBM partial records: 0 (0 repaired)
```

Now let's run the check on both the *WAL* and the *Data* directory:

```
sudo kudu fs check -fs_wal_dir=/var/lib/kudu/tserver
-fs_data_dirs=/var/lib/kudu/tserver
```

In this simple example, we actually get the same output as earlier.

format

This prepares (formats) a brand-new Kudu filesystem.

Remember that this formatting is for the Kudu filesystem, not the operating system's filesystem. Kudu's filesystem is a set of user files and directories sitting on top of the OS filesystem, which means that you already need to have a directory or mount point prepared, with a supporting OS filesystem such as ext3. In our case, the / mount point is already on a basic xfs-formatted filesystem.

Let's see how our / filesystem is mounted currently:

```
$ mount | grep -E '^/dev'
/dev/xvda2 on / type xfs (rw,relatime,seclabel,attr2,inode64,noquota)
```

Here we see that the /dev/xvda2 device mounted on / has been formatted as the xfs filesystem. We can also check the /etc/fstab file for the set of defined mount points.

For our purposes, we next prepare directories for our new Kudu *WAL* and *Data* directories, which we will then format using the Kudu format option:

```
# Create the WAL directory and assign ownership to kudu user
$ sudo mkdir /kudu-wal
$ sudo chown kudu:kudu /kudu-wal
```

```
# Create 8 directories for Data
$ for i in `seq 1 8`; do sudo mkdir /kudu-data$i;sudo chown kudu:kudu
/kudu-data$i; done
```

In this simple example, there's no real benefit to creating eight directories that are mounted on the same underlying disk. This is more relevant when each of these Kudu directories, including the *WAL* directory, are written on a mount point on their own disks.

Let's format these directories now for Kudu use:

```
sudo kudu fs format -fs_wal_dir=/kudu-wal
-fs_data_dirs=/kudu-data1,/kudu-data2,/kudu-data3,/kudu-data4,/kudu-data5,
/kudu-data6,/kudu-data7,/kudu-data8
```

The output you'll see is something along these lines:

```
I0821 22:33:10.068599  3199 env_posix.cc:1455] Raising process file limit from
  1024 to 4096
I0821 22:33:10.068696  3199 file_cache.cc:463] Constructed file cache lbm with
  capacity 1638
I0821 22:33:10.078719  3199 fs_manager.cc:377] Generated new instance metadata
  in path /kudu-data1/instance:
uuid: "a7bc320ed46b47719da6c3b0073c74cc"
format_stamp: "Formatted at 2017-08-22 02:33:10 on ip-172-31-48-12.ec2.internal"
I0821 22:33:10.083366  3199 fs_manager.cc:377] Generated new instance metadata in
  path /kudu-data2/instance:
uuid: "a7bc320ed46b47719da6c3b0073c74cc"
...
I0821 22:33:10.141870  3199 fs_manager.cc:377] Generated new instance metadata in
  path /kudu-wal/instance:
uuid: "a7bc320ed46b47719da6c3b0073c74cc"
format_stamp: "Formatted at 2017-08-22 02:33:10 on ip-172-31-48-12.ec2.internal"
```

Notice that this single filesystem is registered according to a given uuid. In this case, the uuid is a7bc320ed46b47719da6c3b0073c74cc. You also can specify this uuid when creating the formatted data directory.

dump

The dump command enables you to dump various portions of the filesystem.

We begin by dumping the uuid of the filesystem, which we get by specifying the *WAL* and *Data* directories:

```
sudo kudu fs dump uuid -fs_wal_dir=/var/lib/kudu/tserver
```

This will dump a little information, where the relevant last line shows the uuid:

```
....
uuid: "3505a1efac6b4bdc93a5129bd7cf624e"
format_stamp: "Formatted at 2017-08-15 17:08:52 on ip-172-31-48-12.ec2.internal"
3505a1efac6b4bdc93a5129bd7cf624e
```

Next, we want to get more information about this filesystem. We can dump it at the block level and see a lot more information:

```
$ sudo kudu fs dump tree -fs_wal_dir=/var/lib/kudu/tserver
```

This gives us information such as the following:

```
1 data directories: /var/lib/kudu/tserver/data
Total live blocks: 6
Total live bytes: 8947
Total live bytes (after alignment): 32768
Total number of LBM containers: 5 (0 full)
...
uuid: "3505a1efac6b4bdc93a5129bd7cf624e"
format_stamp: "Formatted at 2017-08-15 17:08:52 on ip-172-31-48-12.ec2.internal"
File-System Root: /var/lib/kudu/tserver
|-instance
|-wals/
|----4322392e8d3b49538a959be9d37d6dc0/
|-------wal-000000001
|-------index.000000000
|----15346a340a0841798232f2a3a991c35d/
|-------wal-000000001
|-------index.000000000
|----7eea0cba0b854d28bf9c4c7377633373/
|-------wal-000000001
|-------index.000000000
|-tablet-meta/
|----4322392e8d3b49538a959be9d37d6dc0
|----15346a340a0841798232f2a3a991c35d
|----7eea0cba0b854d28bf9c4c7377633373
|-consensus-meta/
|----4322392e8d3b49538a959be9d37d6dc0
|----15346a340a0841798232f2a3a991c35d
|----7eea0cba0b854d28bf9c4c7377633373
|-data/
|----block_manager_instance
|----35b032f3488e4db390ee3fc3b90249c7.metadata
|----35b032f3488e4db390ee3fc3b90249c7.data
|----eb44ed9bbcce479c89908fbe939ccf49.metadata
|----eb44ed9bbcce479c89908fbe939ccf49.data
|----9e4d11c4b6ac4e1ea140364d171e5e7b.metadata
|----9e4d11c4b6ac4e1ea140364d171e5e7b.data
|----80a281a920fc4c10b79ea7d2b87b8ded.metadata
|----80a281a920fc4c10b79ea7d2b87b8ded.data
|----2f5bc79e814f4a6a98b12a79d5994e99.metadata
|----2f5bc79e814f4a6a98b12a79d5994e99.data
```

You can find the block_id by using the following dump commands on the local or remote replicas. Columns are broken down into blocks which each have their own block ID. In the next section on dumping Tablet information, you can find how to get the block ID, then you can dump the contents in human-readable format with the following command:

```
$ sudo kudu fs dump cfile 0000000000000007 -fs_wal_dir=/var/lib/kudu/tserver
Header:

Footer:
data_type: INT64
encoding: BIT_SHUFFLE
num_values: 1
posidx_info {
  root_block {
    offset: 51
    size: 19
  }
}
validx_info {
  root_block {
    offset: 70
    size: 16
  }
}
compression: NO_COMPRESSION
metadata {
  key: "min_key"
  value: "\200\000\000\000\000\000\000\001"
}
metadata {
  key: "max_key"
  value: "\200\000\000\000\000\000\000\001"
}
is_type_nullable: false
incompatible_features: 0

1
```

As an administrator, this gives visibility into the actual block showing various details about data types, encoding strategies, compression settings, min/max keys and more.

Tablet Replica

You can perform tablet replica operations either locally or remotely by using the local_replica or remote_replica operations, respectively. These operations are used to take a slightly higher up view from the blocks themselves that we saw at the end of the last section. A remote_replica command is useful here because you don't have to log in to each and every machine just to run the commands.

Let's begin by listing the replicas we have on our server:

```
sudo kudu local_replica list -fs_wal_dir=/var/lib/kudu/tserver
...
```

```
4322392e8d3b49538a959be9d37d6dc0
15346a340a0841798232f2a3a991c35d
7eea0cba0b854d28bf9c4c7377633373
```

We can inspect one of these local replicas by dumping information about it. Let's begin with the block_ids themselves:

```
sudo kudu local_replica dump block_ids 15346a340a0841798232f2a3a991c35d
-fs_wal_dir=/var/lib/kudu/tserver
Rowset 0
Column block for column ID 0 (key[int64 NOT NULL]): 0000000000000007
Column block for column ID 1 (ts_val[unixtime_micros NOT NULL]): 0000000000000008
```

We can further dump information about the metadata of the table replica:

```
$ sudo kudu local_replica dump meta 15346a340a0841798232f2a3a991c35d
-fs_wal_dir=/var/lib/kudu/tserver
Partition: HASH (key) PARTITION 1, RANGE (key) PARTITION UNBOUNDED
Table name: python-example Table id: d8f1c3b488c1433294c3daf0af4038c7
Schema (version=0): Schema [
        0:key[int64 NOT NULL],
        1:ts_val[unixtime_micros NOT NULL]
]
Superblock:
table_id: "d8f1c3b488c1433294c3daf0af4038c7"
tablet_id: "15346a340a0841798232f2a3a991c35d"
last_durable_mrs_id: 0
rowsets {
  id: 0
  last_durable_dms_id: -1
  columns {
    block {
      id: 7
    }
    column_id: 0
  }
  columns {
    block {
      id: 8
    }
    column_id: 1
  }
  bloom_block {
    id: 9
  }
}
table_name: "python-example"
schema {
  columns {
    id: 0
    name: "key"
    type: INT64
    is_key: true
```

```
      is_nullable: false
      encoding: AUTO_ENCODING
      compression: DEFAULT_COMPRESSION
      cfile_block_size: 0
    }
    columns {
      id: 1
      name: "ts_val"
      type: UNIXTIME_MICROS
      is_key: false
      is_nullable: false
      encoding: AUTO_ENCODING
      compression: LZ4
      cfile_block_size: 0
    }
  }
  schema_version: 0
  tablet_data_state: TABLET_DATA_READY
  orphaned_blocks {
    id: 10
  }
  partition {
    hash_buckets: 1
    partition_key_start: "\000\000\000\001"
    partition_key_end: ""
  }
  partition_schema {
    hash_bucket_schemas {
      columns {
        id: 0
      }
      num_buckets: 2
      seed: 0
    }
    range_schema {
      columns {
        id: 0
      }
    }
  }
}
```

In this block of replica metadata output, we have preamble content describing the
table itself, such as its name and schema. Next, *rowset* information is provided on a
per-column level followed by a detailed description of the table schema, per column.
The final portion of the dump shows us the state of this tablet, and provides details
about the partitioning schema that this replica uses.

Next, let's go a bit deeper, looking into the rowset itself:

```
$ sudo kudu local_replica dump rowset 15346a340a0841798232f2a3a991c35d
-fs_wal_dir=/var/lib/kudu/tserver
Dumping rowset 0
```

```
------------------------------------------------------------------
   RowSet metadata: id: 0
last_durable_dms_id: -1
columns {
  block {
    id: 7
  }
  column_id: 0
}
columns {
  block {
    id: 8
  }
  column_id: 1
}
bloom_block {
  id: 9
}

   Dumping column block 0000000000000007 for column id 0( key[int64 NOT NULL]):
   ------------------------------------------------------------------
   CFile Header:

   Dumping column block 0000000000000008 for column id 1( ts_val[unixtime_micros
                                                                  NOT NULL]):
   ------------------------------------------------------------------
   CFile Header:
```

We get similar information as in the replica dump, beginning with seeing how the rowset looks per column, and then we gain detailed insight for each column block that exists for the rowset dump.

Finally, we dump out the WAL information for this replica and are privy to seeing a sequence number in the WAL, followed by schema information, compression details, a set of operations that occurred, and information about the minimum and maximum replica indices:

```
$ sudo kudu local_replica dump wals  15346a340a0841798232f2a3a991c35d
-fs_wal_dir=/var/lib/kudu/tserver
Header:
tablet_id: "15346a340a0841798232f2a3a991c35d"
sequence_number: 1
schema {
  columns {
    id: 0
    name: "key"
    type: INT64
    is_key: true
    is_nullable: false
    encoding: AUTO_ENCODING
    compression: DEFAULT_COMPRESSION
    cfile_block_size: 0
```

```
    }
    columns {
      id: 1
      name: "ts_val"
      type: UNIXTIME_MICROS
      is_key: false
      is_nullable: false
      encoding: AUTO_ENCODING
      compression: LZ4
      cfile_block_size: 0
    }
  }
schema_version: 0
compression_codec: LZ4
1.1@6155710131387969536 REPLICATE NO_OP
        id { term: 1 index: 1 } timestamp: 6155710131387969536 op_type:
          NO_OP noop_request { }
COMMIT 1.1
        op_type: NO_OP commited_op_id { term: 1 index: 1 }
1.2@6155710131454771200 REPLICATE WRITE_OP
        Tablet: 15346a340a0841798232f2a3a991c35d
        RequestId: client_id: "1ffdc96b901545468e37569a262d3bd1" seq_no:
          1 first_incomplete_seq_no: 0 attempt_no: 0
        Consistency: CLIENT_PROPAGATED
        op 0: INSERT (int64 key=1, unixtime_micros
                    ts_val=2017-08-16T04:48:38.803992Z)
        op 1: MUTATE (int64 key=1) SET ts_val=2017-01-01T00:00:00.000000Z
COMMIT 1.2
        op_type: WRITE_OP commited_op_id { term: 1 index: 2 } result { ops
          { skip_on_replay: true mutated_stores { mrs_id: 0 } } ops
          { skip_on_replay: true mutated_stores { mrs_id: 0 } } }
2.3@6157789003386167296 REPLICATE NO_OP
        id { term: 2 index: 3 } timestamp: 6157789003386167296 op_type:
          NO_OP noop_request { }
COMMIT 2.3
        op_type: NO_OP commited_op_id { term: 2 index: 3 }
Footer:
num_entries: 6
min_replicate_index: 1
max_replicate_index: 3
```

We can also look at the `remote_replica` command, and what we'll do is copy one of those replicas over to this node.

First, we take a look at the list of tablet servers we have so that we can move a replica from one of those servers to our local server:

```
$ kudu tserver list ip-172-31-48-12
              uuid              |            rpc-addresses
--------------------------------+------------------------------------
 bb50e454938b4cce8a6d0df3a252cd44 | ip-172-31-54-170.ec2.internal:7050
 060a83dd48e9422ea996a8712b21cae4 | ip-172-31-56-0.ec2.internal:7050
```

```
3505a1efac6b4bdc93a5129bd7cf624e | ip-172-31-48-12.ec2.internal:7050
e60fc0618b824f6a994748c053f9f4c2 | ip-172-31-59-149.ec2.internal:7050
```

Now let's do a remote replica listing (Figure 4-13). This is different from a local_replica listing because we see not only the list of tablet IDs, but we see the state, table name, partition, estimated on-disk size, and schema:

```
$ sudo kudu remote_replica list ip-172-31-56-0.ec2.internal:7050
Tablet id: 7eea0cba0b854d28bf9c4c7377633373
State: RUNNING
Table name: python-example-repl2
Partition: HASH (key) PARTITION 3, RANGE (key) PARTITION UNBOUNDED
Estimated on disk size: 310B
Schema: Schema [
        0:key[int64 NOT NULL],
        1:ts_val[unixtime_micros NOT NULL]
]
Tablet id: ca921612aeac4516886f36bab0415749
State: RUNNING
Table name: python-example-repl2
Partition: HASH (key) PARTITION 1, RANGE (key) PARTITION UNBOUNDED
Estimated on disk size: 341B
Schema: Schema [
        0:key[int64 NOT NULL],
        1:ts_val[unixtime_micros NOT NULL]
]
Tablet id: 4e2dc9f0cbde4597a7dca2fd1a05f995
State: RUNNING
Table name: python-example-repl2
Partition: HASH (key) PARTITION 2, RANGE (key) PARTITION UNBOUNDED
Estimated on disk size: 0B
Schema: Schema [
        0:key[int64 NOT NULL],
        1:ts_val[unixtime_micros NOT NULL]
]
Tablet id: 1807d376c9a044daac9b574e5243145b
State: RUNNING
Table name: python-example-repl2
Partition: HASH (key) PARTITION 0, RANGE (key) PARTITION UNBOUNDED
Estimated on disk size: 310B
Schema: Schema [
        0:key[int64 NOT NULL],
        1:ts_val[unixtime_micros NOT NULL]
]
```

For the purpose of simplicity in the following figures, we make note of the last three alphanumeric characters in the Tablet IDs listed in the previous code example so it is easier to identify which tablet we are describing.

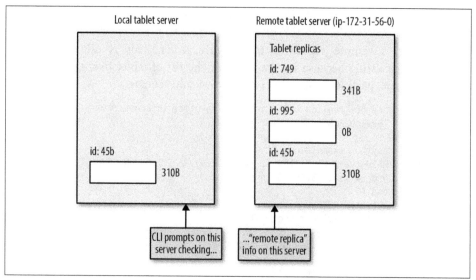

Figure 4-13. Remote replica listing

Copy a remote replica to a local server

To copy a replica from a remote server, you need to stop the local server on which you're running. Then, the copy command is in fact making a connection to the remote, up and running server, and making a copy of the replica locally.

After you're logged into the local server, stop the server by using the following command:

```
sudo systemctl stop kudu-tserver
```

Suppose that we want to copy over Tablet ID 1807d376c9a044daac9b574e5243145b that is on remote_replica ip-172-31-56-0. We already have that on our local replica. Let's see how this works.

```
$ su - kudu
$ kudu local_replica copy_from_remote 1807d376c9a044daac9b574e5243145b
ip-172-31-56-0.ec2.internal:7050 -fs_wal_dir=/var/lib/kudu/tserver

I0821 23:43:38.586378  3078 tablet_copy_client.cc:166] T
1807d376c9a044daac9b574e5243145b P 3505a1efac6b4bdc93a5129bd7cf624e:
Tablet Copy client: Beginning tablet copy session from remote peer at address
  ip-172-31-56-0.ec2.internal:7050
Already present: Tablet already exists: 1807d376c9a044daac9b574e5243145b
```

You must run the `copy_from_remote` command of `local_replica` must be run as the kudu user itself to have appropriate permissions to perform the task. You can't do this as `root` or as a `sudo` user.

The error message is clear that if you have a replica of a given tablet on the remote server but also already present on the local server, it won't actually allow you to copy it—you already have it (Figure 4-14).

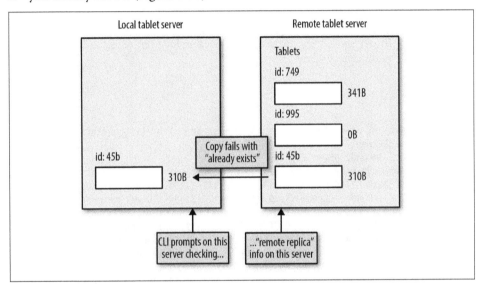

Figure 4-14. Failed copy with an alert that the tablet already exists

Let's now pick a replica that we do not have on our local server. In our case, `PARTITION 1` is found only on the remote server, not locally. It is represented by ID `ca921612aeac4516886f36bab0415749`. Let's try to copy that:

```
$ kudu local_replica copy_from_remote ca921612aeac4516886f36bab0415749
    ip-172-31-56-0.ec2.internal:7050 -fs_wal_dir=/var/lib/kudu/tserver
I0821 23:55:19.530689  3971 tablet_copy_client.cc:166] T
    ca921612aeac4516886f36bab0415749 P 3505a1efac6b4bdc93a5129bd7cf624e:
    Tablet Copy client: Beginning tablet copy session from remote peer at
    address ip-172-31-56-0.ec2.internal:7050
I0821 23:55:19.542532  3971 tablet_copy_client.cc:422] T
    ca921612aeac4516886f36bab0415749 P 3505a1efac6b4bdc93a5129bd7cf624e:
    Tablet Copy client: Starting download of 3 data blocks...
I0821 23:55:19.562101  3971 tablet_copy_client.cc:385] T
    ca921612aeac4516886f36bab0415749 P 3505a1efac6b4bdc93a5129bd7cf624e:
    Tablet Copy client: Starting download of 1 WAL segments...
I0821 23:55:19.566256  3971 tablet_copy_client.cc:292] T
    ca921612aeac4516886f36bab0415749 P 3505a1efac6b4bdc93a5129bd7cf624e:
    Tablet Copy client: Tablet Copy complete. Replacing tablet superblock.
```

We've now copied the data successfully. At this point, we have four replicas of this dataset as it has been active on three replicas already.

However, although the tablet has been copied, it doesn't immediately take part in the Raft consensus. Consequently, it doesn't actually have any role yet; it can be neither a follower nor a leader of this local replica.

Let's take a look at our table again and the specific set of tablets we have. The second column next to the T gives us the tablet ID, whereas the entries in the row give us the replica UUIDs:

In our shell, we've exported the variable KMASTER with the list of Kudu master servers.

```
[ec2-user@ip-172-31-48-12 ~]$ kudu table list $KMASTER -list_tablets
python-example-repl2
T 1807d376c9a044daac9b574e5243145b
  P    060a83dd48e9422ea996a8712b21cae4(ip-172-31-56-0.ec2.internal:7050)
  P(L) e60fc0618b824f6a994748c053f9f4c2(ip-172-31-59-149.ec2.internal:7050)
  P    bb50e454938b4cce8a6d0df3a252cd44(ip-172-31-54-170.ec2.internal:7050)
T ca921612aeac4516886f36bab0415749
  P(L) e60fc0618b824f6a994748c053f9f4c2(ip-172-31-59-149.ec2.internal:7050)
  P    060a83dd48e9422ea996a8712b21cae4(ip-172-31-56-0.ec2.internal:7050)
  P    bb50e454938b4cce8a6d0df3a252cd44(ip-172-31-54-170.ec2.internal:7050)
T 4e2dc9f0cbde4597a7dca2fd1a05f995
  P(L) e60fc0618b824f6a994748c053f9f4c2(ip-172-31-59-149.ec2.internal:7050)
  P    060a83dd48e9422ea996a8712b21cae4(ip-172-31-56-0.ec2.internal:7050)
  P    bb50e454938b4cce8a6d0df3a252cd44(ip-172-31-54-170.ec2.internal:7050)
T 7eea0cba0b854d28bf9c4c7377633373
  P(L) e60fc0618b824f6a994748c053f9f4c2(ip-172-31-59-149.ec2.internal:7050)
  P    060a83dd48e9422ea996a8712b21cae4(ip-172-31-56-0.ec2.internal:7050)
  P    bb50e454938b4cce8a6d0df3a252cd44(ip-172-31-54-170.ec2.internal:7050)
```

Let's disable the tablet ID ca921612aeac4516886f36bab0415749 with replica UUID 060a83dd48e9422ea996a8712b21cae4 so that we can enable it on the new system to which we just copied the replica:

```
#
$ kudu tablet change_config remove_replica $KMASTER
    ca921612aeac4516886f36bab0415749 060a83dd48e9422ea996a8712b21cae4

# Now add the replica on the 12 server
kudu tablet change_config change_replica_type $KMASTER
ca921612aeac4516886f36bab0415749 060a83dd48e9422ea996a8712b21cae4 NON-VOTER

kudu tablet change_config add_replica $KMASTER ca921612aeac4516886f36bab0415749
```

Figure 4-15 depicts what we just performed. We identified the tablet replica we wanted to copy locally. By stopping the local tablet server first, we copied the tablet, disabled the old replica, activated the current one, and then we restart the tablet server.

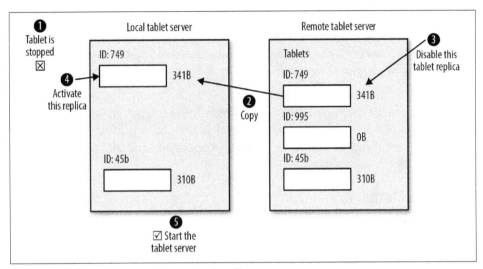

Figure 4-15. Copying a remote replica locally

Deleting a replica

Using the `local_replica delete` option, you can delete a replica manually on a given tablet server. To do so, you first need to stop the tablet server and then carry out the `delete` operation:

```
# Stop the tablet server
sudo service kudu-tserver stop

# List the replicas on your tablet server
sudo kudu local_replica list --fs_wal_dir=/var/lib/kudu/tserver
4322392e8d3b49538a959be9d37d6dc0
15346a340a0841798232f2a3a991c35d
ca921612aeac4516886f36bab0415749

# Delete the one you prefer
sudo kudu local_replica delete 4322392e8d3b49538a959be9d37d6dc0
  --fs_wal_dir=/var/lib/kudu/tserver
uuid: "3505a1efac6b4bdc93a5129bd7cf624e"
format_stamp: "Formatted at 2017-08-15 17:08:52 on ip-172-31-48-12.ec2.internal"
I0915 17:26:11.767314  2780 ts_tablet_manager.cc:1063]
  T 4322392e8d3b49538a959be9d37d6dc0 P 3505a1efac6b4bdc93a5129bd7cf624e:
  Deleting tablet data with delete state TABLET_DATA_TOMBSTONED
I0915 17:26:11.773490  2780 ts_tablet_manager.cc:1075]
  T 4322392e8d3b49538a959be9d37d6dc0 P 3505a1efac6b4bdc93a5129bd7cf624e:
```

```
Tablet deleted. Last logged OpId: 7.8
I0915 17:26:11.773535  2780 log.cc:965]
  T 4322392e8d3b49538a959be9d37d6dc0
  P 3505a1efac6b4bdc93a5129bd7cf624e: Deleting WAL directory at
  /var/lib/kudu/tserver/wals/4322392e8d3b49538a959be9d37d6dc0
```

Notice that the tablet data is actually set to the TABLET_DATA_TOMBSTONED state. We can see from the log message that the WAL has been deleted completely. Data from your replica is likewise cleaned up; however, consensus and tablet metadata information remains by default. This is to ensure that Raft vote durability requirements remain intact.

To fully remove all the metadata as well (which is considered an unsafe operation because if it is not done properly then it may yield harmful side effects), you can add the --clean_unsafe=true option to the delete operation, and all the replica metadata information will be removed.

Consensus Metadata

You can also try metadata for consensus information about replicas.

We can begin by printing replica UUIDs so that we're able to dig into the Raft configuration and dump all the peer UUIDs that exist for a tablet replica.

Let's first list the set of replicas on our host:

```
# List replicas on this tablet server
sudo kudu local_replica list --fs_wal_dir=/var/lib/kudu/tserver
15346a340a0841798232f2a3a991c35d
ca921612aeac4516886f36bab0415749
```

Now we can see the peer UUIDs in Raft's configuration by picking one of the replicas:

```
# Peer UUIDs for Raft configuration
sudo kudu local_replica cmeta print_replica_uuids
  ca921612aeac4516886f36bab0415749
  --fs_wal_dir=/var/lib/kudu/tserver
e60fc0618b824f6a994748c053f9f4c2 060a83dd48e9422ea996a8712b21cae4
  bb50e454938b4cce8a6d0df3a252cd44
```

Hence, we can see three UUIDs of peer replicas. This example is actually from a tombstoned replica. As a result, we can still see the Raft consensus information stored on this tablet server, and we would need to perform a delete with the --clean_unsafe operation in order to fully clean up this information.

You also can rewrite a tablet's Raft configuration by using the rewrite_raft_config operation on the cmeta data. We leave it to you to check the documentation and proceed with caution; this type of action should be performed only by advanced users in situations when the system might be down.

Similarly you can change Raft replication configurations on a remote tablet server. By passing in the remote tablet server, the tablet ID, and the set of peer UUIDs, you can overwrite the Raft consensus configuration. You can use this to recover from problematic scenarios such as a loss of a majority of replicas. But be aware that there is the risk of losing edits. See the kudu `remote_replica unsafe_change_config` operation for details.

Adding and Removing Tablet Servers

A common operation an administrator will want to do properly is to add more nodes to their Kudu cluster. At the same time, there might be circumstances for which we need to remove nodes from the cluster. In this section, we cover the strategy to add and remove tablet servers as required.

Adding Tablet Servers

Adding new tablet servers typically just means installing the necessary binaries for tablet servers and making configuration changes to inform those tablet servers with which master servers it needs to register.

Here is an example of installing binaries. Follow the Quick Install instructions from Chapter 3 to set up the Kudu repository. Then, install only the packages required for the tablet server:

```
sudo yum -y install kudu            # Base Kudu files (all nodes)
sudo yum -y install kudu-tserver    # Kudu tablet server (tablet nodes only)
```

In our three-minute tutorial, we didn't bother to make any adjustments to configuration files, because everything was installed on the localhost. This time, we've installed only the tablet server, with no master server installed on this host. So let's set a few configuration parameters on this tablet server.

You can find the primary file that contains flags and options under */etc/kudu/conf/ tserver.gflagfile*.

Open that file in your favorite editor and append the following line:

```
--tserver_master_addrs=ip-172-31-48-12.ec2.internal:7051
```

Now start the tablet server service itself:

```
sudo systemctl start kudu-tserver
```

Point your browser to the tablet server web UI for the logs to validate that the server attached appropriately, or just take a look at the logs in the terminal directly:

```
sudo vi /var/log/kudu/kudu-tserver.INFO
```

You should see a similar command to the following:

```
sudo grep Register /var/log/kudu/kudu-tserver.INFO
I0816 00:41:36.482281 10669 heartbeater.cc:361] Registering TS with master...
```

While at the top of the log file, you'll see the parameters you specified as flags for the service.

Removing a Tablet Server

Removing a tablet server basically involves decommissioning them than removing the packages associated with Kudu on that node.

To decommission a tablet server gracefully, it is safest to take the following steps:

1. Copy all the replicas from the tablet server to another live tablet server and ensure it is part of the Raft concensus

2. Remove all replicas from the given tablet server

3. Stop the tablet server

4. Remove tablet server binaries

To ensure that no new tablets are being created on the tablet server while performing the decommissioning operation, you will need to simply ensure that no new DDL is taking place at the time of the removal.

You can find the full list of options for configuring tablet servers here (*http:// kudu.apache.org/docs/configuration.html#_configuring_tablet_servers*).

Security

In any serious deployment, regardless of the enterprise size, security can never be an afterthought. Security is typically thought about in the following three ways:

Authentication
A guarantee that the person attempting access is who they say they are.

Authorization
A mode of providing access to the given person, whether that be to a given technology or data.

Encryption
Data flowing over the network and/or stored at rest is encrypted.

We go through some of these concepts using a simple analogy before we get into configuring Kudu with security.

A Simple Analogy

A simple example of authentication in everyday life is handing over your passport when passing through security at an airport. The border guard confirms that you are the passport holder by comparing the photo in the passport with you standing right in front of them. Passing this checkpoint means that you've been "authenticated," or in other words, they have validated that you are who you say you are.

In this airport analogy, as you progress to your gate for boarding, the agents at the gate validate that you indeed are allowed to board the plane. Your boarding pass allows you to board only the airplane for which you have purchased a ticket. This is a form of *authorization* because you are authorized, and authorized only to board that one plane, which is cross-checked by the gate agents.

Now, suppose that you had a letter you were taking to your mom that you wanted to be kept a secret so that only your mom can read it when you reach her. If you were to scramble the contents of your letter while you were still at home, even if someone robbed you on the way to the airport, or someone managed to grab your letter while you were going through customs or boarding the plane, no one would be able to know or steal the contents of your message.

In the world of data management, "boarding the plane" would be the same as access to a database or a table within a database, or a file within a filesystem, for example. Meanwhile, the border guard authenticating you performs the similar job of the industry standard big data strong authentication mechanism, Kerberos. Finally, the scrambled contents of your letter represent encryption in transit, and perhaps at rest, as well, as you leave the letter at your mom's house.

We can further think through this analogy by coming to the realization that authentication is something you, as a client, are responsible for in the sense that you needed to bring your passport with you. Further, you as a client also need to make a judgment call that indeed the border guard is truly a representative of the border patrol for the given country. We intuitively know this based on the uniform or badge they wear. We can then know the agency that issued the border guard's badge from prior knowledge.

Hence, from a "passenger" or "client-side" perspective, there are two pieces of information we have access to on our end:

- A passport proving who we are
- Prior knowledge of the authority that issued the badge and uniform to the border officer

From "airport/airline" or "server-side" perspective, we need to be configured to do the following:

- Agree to allow passport checks as the mode of validating who you are
- Have border guards who wear the right badge and uniform
- Have knowledge about which plane you are allowed to board

These concepts are close enough for what we need to understand when configuring security for Kudu.

On the client side, the client needs to do the following:

- Be Kerberos enabled and have the Kerberos Ticket Granting Ticket (TGT) when accessing Kudu (i.e., the passport)
- Have knowledge of the Certificate Authority (CA) for validating Transport Layer Security (TLS) certificates configured on the Kudu end (i.e., knowledge of the authority for the guard's badge)

On the server side, the server needs to do the following:

- Be enabled for Kerberos authentication (i.e., agree to a passport being the mode of validation and authentication)
- Have TLS certificates that were signed by an appropriate CA (i.e., border guards wearing the right badge and uniform)
- Have an authorization database of who has access to which table, which would typically be done by a service such as Sentry (i.e., knowledge about the plane you're allowed to board, which is stored in a database by the airline)

With this primer under our belts, we can go through the capabilities Kudu has today with regard to security and where it is headed in the near future.

Kudu Security Features

Kudu's support of security features is continually increasing, and at the time of this writing, it supports the following:

- Encryption over the wire, using TLS
- Data at rest encryption
- Kerberos authentication
- Coarse-grained authorization itself
- Finer-grained authorization via Impala
- Log redaction
- Web UI security

Encryption over the wire

Encryption over the wire needs to be looked at from two different perspectives. The first is with *internal* communication between tablet and master servers within the cluster. Kudu has a built-in mechanism to build and issue internal X.509 certificates to all the servers in the cluster. Hence, TLS is the primary mechanism used in encrypting traffic over the wire, internal to the cluster.

These certificates serve a second purpose for intracluster communication. They in fact offer strong authentication using this mechanism so that each server within the cluster can trust that the service connecting to it, whether it be a tablet server or master server, is in fact who they say they are.

Normally, Kerberos is used for authentication, though in this particular case, using the certificate strategy for intracluster communication allows for less load on the Kerberos Key Distribution Center (KDC). This allows for the cluster to scale really well in terms of not having to go to the KDC for each service in the cluster for authentication purposes; rather, they rely on certificates to guarantee authentication for intracluster server communication.

Encryption between Kudu clients and servers is also enabled by using this very same mechanism. Hence, enabling encryption for over-the-wire communication and authentication between servers is as simple as setting the flags:

```
--rpc_authentication=required
--rpc_encryption=required
```

Setting this set of flags simply means setting them as command-line parameters when starting the master and tablet servers or as entries in the flagfile during startup. Kudu services on all nodes must be started with this set of flags to properly take effect.

These flags are set when the master or tablet servers are started. Here is an example specifying them directly in the command-line options, you can also specify them in the gflagfile mentioned by the --flagfile option:

```
kudu-master --rpc_authentication=required --rpc_encryption=required
--master_addresses=... --flagfile=gflagfile
```

Alternatively, if you're running Kudu in Cloudera, it is as simple as setting the enable_security flag in Cloudera Manager for the Kudu service, labeled as "Enable Secure Authentication and Encryption"; the preceding two parameters will be automatically set during startup.

We note here that --rpc_encryption has other valid options such as disabled and optional, though usage of those is not recommended. The optional flag will have Kudu attempt to use encryption, and if it fails will allow unencrypted traffic only from trusted subnets. We leave it to you to look more into these options from the Kudu documentation, as in general, we discourage this practice.

Data-at-rest encryption

Data at rest encryption is not possible at this time by Kudu in and of itself; however, it is fully supported to store data on disks that have been encrypted with full-disk encryption tools such as dm-crypt. Hence, anything read or written to these disks would be encrypted on the fly, and this would be transparent to the Kudu application itself.

Kerberos authentication

You enable Kerberos authentication by selecting the "Enable Secure Authentication and Encryption" flag in Cloudera Manager. A few things need to happen for Kerberos authentication to be enabled. A principal, kudu@ACME.COM, needs to be created in the Kerberos KDC. This name, kudu, is not customizable at the moment. Next, you need to create a keytab file for this principal, and then referenced during the startup options as follows:

```
--keytab_file=<path-to-keytab-file>
```

Enabling Kerberos through Cloudera Manager would create the principal and keytab file and set these automatically on the command-line start options of the Kudu services.

With this enabled, the Kudu service is now only allowing clients to connect who have been appropriately authenticated by Kerberos. However, note that any user who is authenticated by Kerberos can access the cluster at this point. Restricting who has access is what we describe in the next section.

User authorization

With Kerberos enabled, we can be sure that the client authenticating to our service is who they say they are, similar to our earlier analogy that the border guard has checked our passport and validated our identity. At the time of writing, Kudu on its own has two sets of users:

Superuser
Administrative functionality to diagnose or repair issues using the kudu command-line tool.

User
Access and modify all tables and data in a Kudu cluster.

When a distribution such as Cloudera manages the Kudu cluster, you can leave the Superuser parameter blank. This means that the service user that actually launched the Kudu master and tablet servers is allowed to do the administrative functions. In this case, it would simply be the user kudu, especially given that this is the principal name used for Kerberos. If it is managed by a distribution, you should leave this as is, unless there are specific reasons why a user needs to be able to use the command-line tools to fix the Kudu cluster for cases in which you cannot use Cloudera Manager directly.

Next, the list of users who should have access by default is everyone, denoted by an asterisk (*). This is extremely coarse-grained user access at the moment; however, the typical use case might be that Impala queries are coming from external reporting tools. Kudu client API access might be restricted by firewalls, or perhaps we assign a single individual functional ID for Extract, Transform, and Load (ETL) jobs that is allowed to create, load, and manipulate content within Kudu.

Hence, we might only want two users given access to Kudu as a whole, which would include the following:

```
impala
etl_id
```

These parameters are set by the following command-line options, where we introduce the ID mko_adm as being a superuser administrator alongside the kudu ID defined by the service principal that started the kudu daemon:

```
--user_acl=impala,etl_id
--superuser-acl=kudu,mko_adm
```

This type of authorization is certainly coarse at the time of writing; however, back to the idea of Impala being the primary reporting or strategy in querying this table, all the authorization controls in place for Impala would apply. Impala integrates with Sentry for authorization, thus access to Impala tables, databases, and columns is controlled as it is capable of today.

We highlight the idea that it is important to remember the concept of an Impala table on top of Kudu is just that—they are decoupled. This means that although we are granted access to specific tables through Impala, if Kudu access through Kudu client API calls is not properly controlled by other means, users would be able to circumvent Impala altogether to manipulate and access data.

Log redaction

All row data is redacted by default from any Kudu server logs to prevent any leakage of sensitive data. There are two more options available to us when it comes to log redaction:

- Redaction disabled in the web UI, but retained for server logs
- Disable redaction altogether

You can set these by making the following adjustments:

```
--redact=log : No redaction in web UI, but server logs still are redacting
    sensitive data
--redact=none: No redaction performed anywhere (not recommended unless debugging!)
```

Web UI security

Web UI security includes the ability to enable TLS for encrypting all traffic to and from clients connecting to the web UI. You need to prepare certificates in Privacy-Enhanced Mail (PEM) format, together with private keys, key passwords (password is emitted by running this specified command), and CA files, which you can set by using the following parameters:

```
--webserver-certificate-file=<path-to-cert-pem>
--webserver-private-key-file=<path-to-key-pem>
--webserver-private-key-password-cmd=<password-cmd>
```

Although TLS is enabled for encrypting traffic over the wire for the web UI, authorization for who is allowed access to this web UI is not controlled, (as of this writing) by Kerberos (which is typically done through SPNEGO).

Until access is restricted, you might decide to fully disable the web server itself by using this command:

```
--webserver-enabled=false
```

It is important to realize that doing this will also disable REST API endpoints that yield metrics for Kudu, which will have an impact on monitoring systems that you might have set up to monitor Kudu.

Basic Performance Tuning

As with any storage system, there can be numerous in-depth performance tuning strategies to keep in mind. Kudu is still in its infancy, but there are a few areas of performance tuning that as an administrator you should understand.

Thus far, a lot has been discussed about the type of underlying storage to make use of for the WALs and storage directories. In the chapters that follow, we take a closer look at schema design, which is absolutely critical to getting appropriate performance for your workloads.

From an administrator's perspective there are a few tunables to keep in mind that we list here, but we acknowledge that it is not an exhaustive list by any means. It is also very important to recognize when the performance bottleneck is actually on the server side of Kudu rather than the client. Sometimes, it is the clients that do not have enough resources (CPU or memory) or enough parallelism to drive the Kudu server to its limits.

From a high-level perspective, there are three primary areas of focus when it comes to tuning for performance:

- Amount of memory assigned to Kudu
- Appropriate partitioning strategies used (as mentioned, this is discussed in future chapters)
- The number of maintenance manager threads

Kudu Memory Limits

Kudu is built from the ground up in C++, using efficient and effective memory management techniques. Although it is meant to be lean, it is still worthwhile to provide Kudu with as much memory as you can allow in the cluster.

In multitenant clusters—and in this case, multitenant means various services all deployed in your big data environment such as HDFS, HBase, Impala, YARN, Spark —you might need to carefully design carving out memory appropriately for each of the services.

Here's the parameter to adjust:

```
--memory_limit_hard_bytes
```

In production environments, you should consider starting this value between 24 GB and 32 GB. You can certainly go higher for these memory settings as well.

Maintenance Manager Threads

Maintenance manager threads are background threads that perform various tasks. They do work such as performing memory management by specifically flushing data from memory to disk (thereby switching from the row-oriented in-memory format of records to a column-oriented on disk format), improving overall read performance or freeing up disk space. Work will be scheduled to these threads whenever a thread is made available.

Row-oriented data is very easy to write out because very little processing is needed to write out a row. Row-oriented means that the data in that row has nothing to do with data in another row. For this reason, it is going to be a very fast write-oriented format. Column-oriented data is more difficult to write fast because it needs more processing to get a row into this format. As a result, column-oriented datasets are faster on reads. When Kudu holds data in memory, waiting for it to be flushed to disk, it is stored in write-optimized row format. However, after it is flushed to disk by the maintenance manager thread, it is then converted into columnar storage, optimized for aggregate read queries.

These are typically set according to the number of data drives that are assigned on a given tablet server. If there are 12 drives on a tablet server, we should set approximately four threads, or one-third the number of spinning disks. The faster the disks are, however, the more threads you can push. Starting from a number of one-third, it is safe to push this number in the range of the number of disks – 1. This is a general recommendation; you will need to test this for the given workload you are tuning. This is more to say do not leave this to the default of one thread, but also do not go into the many tens of threads set for this parameter.

Here's the parameter in question:

```
--maintenance_manager_num_threads
```

Monitoring Performance

Kudu's web UI provides a JSON metrics page that can help you to easily and quickly zero in on certain performance metrics that might indicate a performance bottleneck.

JSON format metrics hook nicely into various dashboarding-type utilities and tools to provide insight as to what is going on in the system.

Getting Ahead and Staying Out of Trouble

As an administrator, it is a often a great idea to try to get ahead of having trouble with your cluster.

We make a few recommendations in this section to help guide you along.

Avoid Running Out of Disk Space

There are two parameters to keep in mind when trying to avoid running out of disk space. Any software platform may have undesired behavior, so there are a few parameters to stay ahead of the curve:

```
--fs_data_dirs_reserved_bytes
--fs_wal_dir_reserved_bytes
```

The default value for these is at 1% of disk space being reserved on the data and WAL directory filesystems for non-Kudu usage. Setting this close to the 5% range (though the parameter itself is set in number of bytes, not percentages, so you need to preform your own calculations) is one area to start with.

Disk Failures Tolerance

Kudu is a quickly evolving product, and is now resilient with sustaining disk failures occurring on tablet servers. Kudu master servers are not yet resilient to sustaining disk failures. As a result, when a disk fails, the entire Kudu master server is not usable.

Tablet servers are tolerant to disk failures; however, if a failure happens on a disk where the WALs or tablet metadata is stored, it will still incur a crash. We leave it to you to stay on top of developments of Kudu when it comes to tolerance levels as the product continues to mature.

Tablet data will actually be striped across multiple disks that are assigned to a tablet server. The default value is 3, and if the value is set to the number of data directories or greater, data will be striped across all of the available disks on the system. If fewer data directories are assigned by tablet, there will be less chance of all tablets on a given tablet server being affected if a drive were to fail (given that data might not be striped on the disk for all tablets existing on the tablet server).

Following is the parameter that controls the number of data directories targeted for a given tablet replica:

```
--fs_target_data_dirs_per_tablet
```

Backup

Core backup functionality is still coming to Kudu, but even if it does shortly, it is still worth thinking about the various strategies that could be employed for backing up data.

Using MapReduce, Spark, or Impala, you could read Kudu tables and write them out to HDFS, preserving the schema but writing in Parquet format. After it is in HDFS, data can be shipped to other clusters in disaster recovery zones, or put in the cloud with the distcp utility, or even backed up with Cloudera's Backup Disaster Recovery (BDR) tool (which maintains table metadata as well among other benefits).

Another way to think about it is to ingest data immediately into two separate data-centers, especially if data is streaming in. Of course, you have to account for any outages in any of the Kudu clusters you're writing to, or even the speeds at which the tables are being populated because the two clusters might be out of synchronization as to how far they got in writing their data. Depending on the use case, this might be sufficient without much synchronization at all.

Conclusion

In this chapter, we covered some common administrator tasks when operating Kudu. We helped administrators plan their environments, discussed the web UI, and went through a slew of CLI commands with which administrators should become familiar. We provided introductory material on enabling security, common scenarios administrators need to perform such as adding and removing nodes and wrapped up by talking about basic performance tuning and tips on avoiding pitfalls. Next, we focus on the needs of the developer; namely, how to get up and running quickly as a developer of a new Kudu application using your programming language and framework of choice.

## CHAPTER 5

Common Developer Tasks for Kudu

At its very core, Apache Kudu is a highly resilient, distributed, fault-tolerant storage engine that manages structured data really well. Moving data *into* Kudu and getting it *out* is meant to be done easily and efficiently through simple-to-understand APIs.

For the developer, you have several choices in how you could interact with the data you store in Kudu. Client-side APIs are provided for the following programming languages:

- C++
- Java
- Python

Compute frameworks such as MapReduce and Spark are also available when interacting with Kudu. MapReduce, using the Java client, has a native Kudu input format, whereas Spark's API provides a specialized Kudu Context together with deep integration with Spark SQL.

Providing SQL access to Kudu is a natural fit given that Kudu stores data in a structured, strongly typed fashion. Thus, as of today, not only can you use Spark SQL to access and manipulate your data, but also Apache Impala. Impala is an open source, native analytic database for Hadoop and is shipped by multiple Hadoop distributions. It, too, provides a clean abstraction of tables that can exist in Kudu, Hadoop Distributed File System (HDFS), HBase, or cloud-based object stores like Amazon Web Services Simple Storage Service (Amazon S3).

In this chapter, we dive into the various client-side APIs, including Spark, and then round out the chapter discussing how Impala's integration with Kudu can be used for many types of use cases. All code snippets described in this chapter are available in our GitHub repository (*http://bit.ly/gswk-ch5*).

Client API

Client APIs have a general workflow and set of objects in common for which a client application needs to be designed. Regardless of the language being used, you obtain instances of these objects in order to define, manipulate, and interact with data stored in Kudu.

Kudu Client

The Kudu Client is created by supplying a list of Kudu master addresses. This object is used to perform the following operations:

- Check for table existence
- Issue Data Definition Language (DDL) operations such as create, delete, and alter table
- Obtain a reference to a Kudu Table object

Thus, you can consider it your primary entry point to interacting with Kudu. After the Table object reference is obtained, you can begin manipulating content within the table.

Kudu Table

A reference to the Kudu Table object allows us in general to perform the following operations:

- Insert/delete/update/upsert rows
- Scan rows

Tables will have a specific schema with strongly typed columns and partitioning strategies which also need to be specified by particular objects.

Kudu DDL

To define a new Kudu table, you need to define a schema. This Kudu Schema object includes column names, their types, nullability, and default values.

Next, you need to define a partitioning method. Kudu supports multiple approaches to partitioning, including partitioning by range and/or by hash value. For this, we define a Kudu Partial Row object.

Finally, we have a Kudu Table Creator object that uses the builder pattern to make it easier to supply all the bits needed to define your table.

To summarize, the set of objects needed to actually create your table include the following:

Kudu Schema
    Defining your columns

Kudu Partial Row
    Defining your partitioning columns

Kudu Table Creator
    Builder pattern implementation for defining your table

Kudu Scanner Read Modes

Scanning through your data is a common practice, and there are a number of important read modes to be familiar with when opening up a scan operation:

- READ_LATEST
- READ_AT_SNAPSHOT
- READ_YOUR_WRITES

READ_LATEST always returns the committed writes at the time the request was received. If we thought of this in Atomicity, Consistency, Isolation, Durability (ACID) terms, it would be the same as isolation mode, "Read Committed"; and this is the default mode. It is not a repeatable read, because data can continually be inserted and/or committed from the last time you performed your scan, so the data coming back could be different each time.

READ_AT_SNAPSHOT allows for a timestamp to be provided, and will attempt to perform the read at that time. If no timestamp is provided, it will take the current time as the "snapshot." Hence, future reads of this dataset should return the exact same set of rows. This particular read mode might incur latency penalties because it needs to wait for in-flight transactions that are taking place *prior* to the given timestamp to complete, before this scan returns. In ACID terms again, this is closer to resembling "Repeatable Read" isolation mode. Meanwhile, if all writes are made consistent (by external mechanisms), this would result in isolation mode, "Strict Serializable."

The newest addition at the time of this writing is READ_YOUR_WRITES, where the read knows *all* the writes and reads made from this client's session. It ensures both read-your-writes and read-your-reads session guarantees while minimizing latency caused by waiting for outstanding write transactions to complete. This mode once again will return different results potentially each time you run this scan because additional writes might have occurred in the meantime. This is an experimental feature for now, but watch for it becoming a stabilized feature in future releases.

C++ API

Kudu is written in C++, whereas most of the traditional Hadoop ecosystem components are Java Virtual Machine–based services. This allows for many optimizations, including not having to rely on garbage collection and having efficient memory and CPU utilization.

The benefit of writing a client application in C++ is that you will be a first-class citizen, with access to the latest and greatest features of Kudu at all times. Your application can likewise be lean in terms of resource utilization and more.

You can always look up the latest C++ API in the documentation (*https://kudu.apache.org/cpp-client-api/*).

Let's run through a few examples (the code snippets are available in our GitHub repository (*https://github.com/kudu-book/getting-started-kudu/tree/master/chapter5/src/kudu/c*)). Even before we begin we include a number of key API header files:

```
#include "kudu/client/callbacks.h"
#include "kudu/client/client.h"
#include "kudu/client/row_result.h"
#include "kudu/client/stubs.h"
#include "kudu/client/value.h"
#include "kudu/common/partial_row.h"
```

The key files we're interested in include *client.h* and *partial_row.h* as we define our tables.

We begin by creating and connecting with a KuduClient object, using the builder pattern supplied by the API:

```
// Create and connect a client
shared_ptr<KuduClient> client;
KuduClientBuilder()
    .add_master_server_addr(masterHost)
    .default_admin_operation_timeout(MonoDelta::FromSeconds(10))
    .Build(&client);
```

We can see that we pass in the set of master servers in the already defined variable masterHost, which should be a comma-delimited list of master servers. If you deviate from using the default port number for the master servers, you need to specify them, as well, after each master hostname.

We can use the KuduClient reference to check the existence of a table and delete the table if it exists. Here is an example:

```
shared_ptr<KuduTable> table;
Status s = client->OpenTable(kTableName, &table);
if (s.ok()) {
```

```
    client->DeleteTable(kTableName);
}
else if (s.IsNotFound()) {
    // Decide what to do if the table is not found
}
else {
    // Handle any other errors
}
```

Notice that in this case we are introduced to the Status object, which is a worthwhile class to look into to be familiar with the various return types and codes that are available to you as you check the responses from the Kudu server in your client code.

Using the Builder pattern, we begin to define our schema:

```
KuduSchema schema;
KuduSchemaBuilder sb;
sb.AddColumn("id")         ->
Type(KuduColumnSchema::INT32)->NotNull()->PrimaryKey();
sb.AddColumn("lastname") ->Type(KuduColumnSchema::STRING)->NotNull();
sb.AddColumn("firstname")->Type(KuduColumnSchema::STRING)->NotNull();
sb.AddColumn("city")       ->
Type(KuduColumnSchema::STRING)->NotNull()->
    Default(KuduValue::CopyString("Toronto"));
```

The Builder pattern enables us to continually add new columns programmatically, specifying the column name, the type, nullability, and default values, as well as the primary key for the table.

Now we pass KuduSchema pointer into the Builder's Build function to actually populate our object:

```
sb.Build(&schema)
```

Next, we create an array, or vector in this case, of a set of KuduPartialRow objects. Each partial row is retrieved from the schema object we defined earlier. A partial row just represents a row with a schema from your table, and you can supply a value to one or more columns. In this context of defining a table, we're really picking the column that will be our partitioning key column. Along with it we supply values for this partitioning key column that will specify where the splits are defined for the partitioned table:

```
vector<const KuduPartialRow *> splits;
KuduPartialRow *row = schema.NewRow();
row->SetInt32("id", 1000);
splits.push_back(row);
row = schema.NewRow();
row->SetInt32("id", 2000);
splits.push_back(row);
row = schema.NewRow();
row->SetInt32("id", 3000);
splits.push_back(row);
```

As each partial row is added into the splits vector, we have our ranges defined for the partitioning scheme we're after in this example.

Next, we need a vector of column names that will represent our range-partitioned column. This list must match the column defined in the splits we just designated:

```
vector<string> columnNames;
columnNames.push_back("id");
```

Taking all the pieces we've built thus far, we can finally call into our KuduClient table creator and define our table:

```
KuduTableCreator *tableCreator = client->NewTableCreator();
s = tableCreator->table_name(kTableName)
    .schema(&schema)
    .set_range_partition_columns(columnNames)
    .split_rows(splits)
    .num_replicas(1)
    .Create();
```

We can see this Builder pattern accepts the table name, the schema we defined (including the primary key), the set of range partition column names followed by the row splits, the number of replicas we want for this table, and finally the Create function to actually define the table in Kudu.

Python API

The Python API is really simply an interface to the C++ Client API. It is easiest to get started by simply installing from PyPI. If you want to install from source, you will be required to install Cython. More on this later. The full code example described in this section is available in our GitHub repository (*https://github.com/kudu-book/getting-started-kudu/tree/master/chapter5/src/kudu/python*).

Preparing the Python Development Environment

In two simple steps, we get off to the races:

1. Install the C++ client libraries and headers

2. Install the kudu-python PyPI libraries

To install the C++ client libraries and headers, you just need the following pair of packages:

```
sudo yum -y install kudu-client-devel kudu-client0
```

For more information, see "Quick Install: Three Minutes or Less" on page 41.

Next, we install pip, though we leave it to you to look up the latest pip documentation (*https://pip.pypa.io/en/stable/installing*).

Install the kudu-python package using pip:

```
sudo pip install kudu-python
```

Our examples run with Python 3.5. We install Python 3.5 by compiling from source. Remember when doing so to install the following additional libraries before compiling Python 3.5 to make sure that pip3 is successfully installed, as well:

```
yum -y install zlib-devel bzip2-devel sqlite sqlite-devel openssl-devel
```

After installing Python 3, install the kudu-python packages:

```
sudo pip3 install kudu-python
```

Python Kudu Application

Python on Kudu applications begin by importing the most common libraries:

```
import kudu
from kudu.client import Partitioning
```

All Python Kudu applications need a client object defined by establishing a connection with a Kudu server. The Kudu server simply needs a list of Kudu master servers and for you to specify the port number in the API, as shown here:

```
client = kudu.connect(host=kuduMaster, port=7051)
```

From there, we will define a table by using the Builder pattern derived from the Kudu schema_builder API call. The first thing we do with the builder is define our columns. We give a few examples of what can be defined in these columns in a moment. Notable elements include the capability to provide column names and types, default values, and nullability, but even more interesting is on a per-column level specifying the compression, encoding, and block size values:

```
builder = kudu.schema_builder()

builder.add_column('lastname').type(
            'string').default('doe').compression('snappy').encoding(
            'plain').nullable(False)
builder.add_column('firstname').type(
            'string').default('jane').compression('zlib').encoding(
            'plain').nullable(False).block_size(20971520)
```

You can also define a new column by specifying parameters directly into the add_column method, as opposed to the dot notation used in the previous example:

```
builder.add_column('ts_val',
                type_=kudu.unixtime_micros,
                nullable=False, compression='lz4')
```

After we define the columns, we define the primary key columns and actually call the build function to get back a kudu.schema object:

```
builder.set_primary_keys(['lastname', 'state_prov', 'key'])
schema = builder.build()
```

As we think about partitioning strategies, in this example we look at defining both a hash-partitioned column together with a set of range-partitioned columns. Hash partitions need to know how many buckets to partition the data into. Meanwhile, range partitions actually need to have the ranges defined. By default, the lower bound of the range is *inclusive*, whereas the upper range is *exclusive*:

```
partitioning = Partitioning().add_hash_partitions(
                column_names=['state_prov'], num_buckets=3, seed=13)

partitioning.set_range_partition_columns('lastname')
partitioning.add_range_partition(['A'], ['E'])
partitioning.add_range_partition(['E'], ['Z'], upper_bound_type='inclusive')
```

We are now all set to create our table; passing in the table name, schema, partitioning schema, and the number of replicas for our tablets:

```
client.create_table(tableName, schema, partitioning, 1)
```

To insert rows into the table, we use the client object again to get a handle for our table and for the given session with which we'll be writing. There are certain properties available with our session such as timeout values, flush strategies, and more:

```
table = client.table(tableName)
session = client.new_session()
session.set_flush_mode(kudu.FLUSH_MANUAL)
session.set_timeout_ms(3000)
```

As we prepare our insert values for the table, we can issue the apply method on the session for the operation. However, depending on the flush mode, nothing might actually be triggered on the Kudu server. Because we decided on a manual flush mode strategy in this case, we would keep applying numerous inserts but really have them all done in one shot:

```
op = table.new_insert({'lastname'  : 'Smith',
                       'state_prov': 'ON',
                       'firstname' : 'Mike',
                       'key'       : 1,
                       'ts_val'    : datetime.utcnow()})
                       session.apply(op)
```

By specifying a set of key–value pairs representing the column and values we are specifying for the insert, we have applied the row to our session, but it has yet to be flushed out. We can perform the preceding operation several times, and if a specific column is *not* specified in the list of key-value pairs, it will automatically be given the default value or null. In the case that null is not allowed and no default is specified, it might be that you must specify the column; otherwise, the insert will fail altogether.

When we're finally ready to have our content flushed, we can call the flush method directly on the session:

```
session.flush()
```

This is where exceptions will potentially be thrown and errors can be handled as appropriate:

```
except kudu.KuduBadStatus as e:
        (errorResult, overflowed) = session.get_pending_errors()
        print("Insert row failed: {} (more pending errors? {})".format(
            errorResult, overflowed))
```

Similar to how the earlier insert operations were performed by calling new_insert, there are a number of other operations you can do, each time specifying the key followed by the values, each in key–value pairs.

Here are the full set of operations:

Insert
    Using the new_insert API call

Upsert
    Using the new_upsert API call—inserts the record if it does not exist; otherwise, if it does exist, it will update the row with the new values provided

Update
    Using the new_update API call

Delete
    Using the new_delete API call

Hence, the set of rows you'd like to insert, upsert, update, or delete essentially requires having a list of the keys of the rows you're modifying. For delete operations, there is no need to specify values of other columns that are not part of the key. Meanwhile, rows that are being updated will update the entire row with the values supplied. For example, assume the row you're updating has the following:

keycol	col1	col2	col3
id1	3	hi	go

Then, update the row as so:

```
table.new_update ({'keycol':'id1', 'col1':5})
```

You update the entire row with the values you specified. Because no value was specified for col2 or col3, you end up with null values in those fields. The final state of the row would now look like this:

keycol	col1	col2	col3
id1	5	-	-

If the intent is to preserve the values that were there prior to your update, you need to first perform a fetch of the row with that ID, and with the row returned, use it to perform the update, by simply modifying the one column.

Java

Java is a first-class citizen in the Hadoop ecosystem, and it is no wonder that it is likely to be used when interacting with Kudu. In the example application we walk through, we first talk a little about setting up the necessary dependencies. There are two schools of thought around building Java JAR files in the sense of whether they should be uber Java ARchives (JARs) or non-uber JARs. The full code example is available in our GitHub repository (*https://github.com/kudu-book/getting-started-kudu/tree/master/chapter5/src/kudu/java*).

Uber JARs have the advantage of being completely self-contained, regardless of the environment you're running in, and they are typically implemented using shading to ensure that libraries bundled in your application do not conflict with any libraries found in the environment in which you're running.

Non-uber JARs have the benefit of using the libraries that are already in your environment; are extremely lean because they contain only the code belonging to your application; and, as long as you make API references that belong in the distribution of Kudu you're running, your application will continually be *upgraded* as Kudu is upgraded.

In our examples, we demonstrate using non-uber JARs because they are easily shipped around to various clusters, quick and easy to compile, and are more easily integrated into your existing environment.

See the example *pom.xml* file we provide for details, but we begin by setting up a few key dependencies of which you should be aware.

The set of plug-ins we employ in our standard Java application for Kudu include the following:

- `maven-compiler-plugin`
- `maven-shade-plugin`

- `maven-surefire-plugin`

These plug-ins allow us to compile our code and share any libraries if we need to, and include unit testing for our code.

Next, we just need to include access to our Kudu client. Currently, we have the Kudu client libraries available in two ways, the libraries supplied by Apache and those supplied by Cloudera. If you are running Kudu in an environment with Cloudera's distribution of Hadoop, create dependencies specific to the version of CDH you are running:

```
<dependency>
  <groupId>org.apache.kudu</groupId>
  <artifactId>kudu-client</artifactId>
  <version>1.5.0-cdh5.13.1</version>
  <scope>provided</scope>
</dependency>
```

You can see the other dependencies for logging and unit testing in the full Project Object Model (POM) file we provide in the code repository for the book.

Java Application

We start our Java application by importing the following set of key classes:

```
import org.apache.kudu.ColumnSchema;
import org.apache.kudu.Schema;
import org.apache.kudu.Type;
import org.apache.kudu.client.*;
```

Next, with a comma-separated list of master server hosts, we get a client connection:

```
KuduClient client = new KuduClient.KuduClientBuilder(KUDU_MASTER).build();
```

The first thing we will do in our example is to define a set of columns using the `ColumnSchemaBuilder` API calls:

```
List<ColumnSchema> columns = new ArrayList(2);
    columns.add(new ColumnSchema.ColumnSchemaBuilder("key", Type.INT32)
        .key(true)
        .build());
    columns.add(new ColumnSchema.ColumnSchemaBuilder("value", Type.STRING)
        .build());
```

So we have two columns, a key column and `value` column. We can now create our schema object out of the columns defined:

```
Schema schema = new Schema(columns);
```

For our range-partitioned column, we define a list of the partition range keys we're interested in:

```
List<String> rangeKeys = new ArrayList<>();
    rangeKeys.add("key");
```

At this point, we have the information we need to create our table; namely, the table name, schema, and range partition information. Let's create the table:

```
client.createTable(tableName, schema,
            new CreateTableOptions().setRangePartitionColumns(rangeKeys));
```

After we've created the table, we set up sessions to start setting ourselves up for inserts. Begin by opening the table from your client connection. Next, create a new session that you will work with, where the session accepts values such as timeout settings and flush strategies:

```
KuduTable table = client.openTable(tableName);
    KuduSession session = client.newSession();
```

With our session in place, we can set up objects for inserts. Java has a newInsert() API call:

```
Insert insert = table.newInsert();
```

The general idea is that after we have an Insert object, we *fetch* a row from it, which of course at this stage will be an empty row. All it contains is a schema associated with that row, and an API that we can use to *populate* the row with values we're interested in populating:

```
PartialRow row = insert.getRow();
    row.addInt(0, i);
    row.addString(1, "value " + i);
    session.apply(insert);
```

Depending on your session object properties, the row might or might not be flushed to the Kudu servers. You can call the flush function on the session object to trigger a flush, or leave it to be done automatically according to the policy specified.

When querying a table in Kudu using the Java API, we build up a specific scanner on the table. Using the builder pattern even for the scanner, we also want to give it a set of columns we would like to project (i.e., the columns typically specified in the select clause of a SQL query):

```
// Set the columns we'd like to project
List<String> projectColumns = new ArrayList<>(1);
    projectColumns.add("value");
// Build the scanner on the table
KuduScanner scanner = client.newScannerBuilder(table)
        .setProjectedColumnNames(projectColumns)
        .build();
```

At this stage, we have a scanner that, although we have more rows, we can loop through and continually get back a row result iterator that we can scan through:

```
while (scanner.hasMoreRows()) {
    RowResultIterator results = scanner.nextRows();
    while (results.hasNext()) {
      RowResult result = results.next();
      System.out.println(result.getString(0));
    }
}
```

You also can call this same Java API from Scala applications as usual, although in the context of big data, we usually turn to Spark to process the data at scale.

Running your Java application would then look similar to the following:

```
java -cp "kudu-java-client-1.0.jar:/opt/cloudera/parcels/CDH/jars/ \
  kudu-client-1.5.0-cdh5.13.1.jar: \
  /opt/cloudera/parcels/CDH/jars/kudu-client-tools-1.5.0-cdh5.13.1.jar" \
  -DkuduMaster=mladen-secure-kudu-8,mladen-secure-kudu-9,mladen-secure-kudu-10 \
  org.apache.gettingstartedkudu.examples.KuduJavaExample
```

The key component of this command is that we're setting the classpath to specify the *.jar* file compiled by our application, namely, kudu-java-client-1.0.jar in this case, followed by a colon-delimited list of the following JARs:

- kudu-client
- kudu-client-tools

In this example, we point to the Cloudera distribution of where the Kudu libraries are installed. But similarly for a standalone installation of Kudu, you would find those same libraries and ensure that they are in your classpath.

The -D flag of specifying master servers is specific to our application example, then we follow that with the main class, which would then be followed by any arguments as required.

Spark

Kudu has Spark-specific libraries available for developers to use with integration directly with Spark's Dataset and Dataframe frameworks. It can also hook into the Resilient Distributed Dataset (RDD) framework directly, if desired. The full code snippet is available in our code repository (*https://github.com/kudu-book/getting-started-kudu/tree/master/chapter5/src/kudu/spark*).

You can write your Spark applications in Java or Scala for Kudu integration, though at the time of writing, PySpark is not available.

When Spark tasks are scanning Kudu tables, you can schedule tasks to read from both leader as well as nonleader replicas. This is a positive performance gain given that scheduled tasks can be more easily scheduled to read data locally (as opposed to being able to read only from leader replicas, which was the case prior to Kudu v1.7).

We use maven as the example to compile our Spark application, using the following three plug-ins in our *pom.xml* file to get us what we need:

- `maven-compiler-plugin`
- `maven-shade-plugin`
- `maven-scala-plugin`

The compiler and shade plug-ins are typically for any Java application, whereas we add the Scala plug-in specifically to compile our Scala code.

Kudu can run on both Spark 1.6 as well as Spark 2, though in our examples, we focus on Spark 2. With Spark 2, it is also mandatory to use the libraries that are specifically using the 2.11 version of Scala, as opposed to the older 2.10. See the example *pom.xml* file for details, but the following dependencies are required to run SparkSQL in particular with Kudu.

`kudu-client`
: The same client we used for the Java API.

`kudu-spark2_2.11`
: The Spark2 bindings we have for Spark on Kudu.

The rest of the dependencies are typical for Spark applications and include:

`scala-library`
: Libraries for Scala code development

`spark-core_2.11`
: Spark core libraries that are mandatory

`spark-sql_2.11`
: Spark SQL-specific libraries

`spark-hive_2.11`
: Spark Hive libraries, for accessing and working with the Hive metastore

The Kudu-specific imports that we require in our Spark application include the following:

```
import org.apache.kudu.spark.kudu._
import org.apache.kudu.client._
```

From there, we begin our Spark application as usual by setting up a Spark session:

```
val spark = SparkSession.builder.appName("Spark on Kudu Getting Started")
    .enableHiveSupport().getOrCreate()
```

Spark on Kudu is different than the other APIs that typically just jump into obtaining your client connection through some sort of Kudu client object. In Spark, we instead set up a KuduContext object that will handle clients and sessions under the covers for us at scale across the cluster.

The KuduContext takes as input a comma-delimited list of master servers with port numbers (port numbers not required if you're using the default) and a reference to the Spark context:

```
val kuduMasters = Seq(master1, master2, master3).mkString(",")

// Create an instance of a KuduContext
val kuduContext = new KuduContext(kuduMasters, spark.sparkContext)
```

Next, we store a set of Kudu options that are reusable across multiple operations as a Map[String, String] containing key–value pairs that can pass parameters down to different operations. We begin by specifying the Kudu table and masters that we're working with:

```
val kuduOptions: Map[String, String] = Map(
      "kudu.table"  -> kuduTableName,
      "kudu.master" -> kuduMasters)
```

The Kudu Context gives us the ability to easily check for the existence of a table and allows us to delete tables, as well:

```
if (kuduContext.tableExists(kuduTableName)) {
    kuduContext.deleteTable(kuduTableName)
}
```

Creating a table begins by defining a schema. We define a schema just like we would for a regular Spark DataFrame. We specify a StructType followed by a set of fields of type StructField that takes as input the column name, type, and nullability flags:

```
val kuduTableSchema = StructType(
//          column name    type          nullable
StructField("name", StringType , false) ::
StructField("age" , IntegerType, true ) ::
StructField("city", StringType , true ) :: Nil)
```

Next we need a list of column names that will make up the primary key. In our example, we have just a single column for the primary key called name:

```
val kuduPrimaryKey = Seq("name")
```

Partition information and number of replicas are then specified in a Kudu Table Options object:

```
val kuduTableOptions = new CreateTableOptions()
    kuduTableOptions.
      setRangePartitionColumns(List("name").asJava).
      setNumReplicas(3)
```

What's important to note about the `CreateTableOptions` call is that the range partition column list needs to be a Java-based list, not a Scala-based list. Hence, the requirement to include the `.asJava` call to our list of range-partitioned columns.

Now we're ready to actually create our table, making a call through the Kudu Context API again:

```
kuduContext.createTable(
        // Table name, schema, primary key and options
        kuduTableName, kuduTableSchema, kuduPrimaryKey, kuduTableOptions)
```

The Kudu Context allows more operations directly through it where we supply the Kudu table name together with the DataFrame we would like to write out or perform an operation with. Here are some sample API calls on the Kudu Context object:

- kuduContext.insertRows

- kuduContext.deleteRows

- kuduContext.upsertRows

- kuduContext.updateRows

For the insert, upsert, and update API calls, a DataFrame with the keys and values need to be specified together with the table you're operating on. However, for delete, you need to have only a DataFrame of keys.

Now, most Spark application and integration patterns do not require an extra object like the Kudu Context object in order to perform Spark applications. Instead the integration is within the DataFrame objects you already have in your Spark applications. It is no different with Kudu where, by specifying the Kudu options we mentioned earlier (the `Map[String, String]` set of options), we can make calls such as the following:

```
customersAppendDF.write.options(kuduOptions).mode("append").kudu
```

In this very succinct, elegant way, we have specified a DataFrame, instructed it to write, using the Kudu options (that give us the master servers for the Kudu cluster and the Kudu table name), and instruct it to insert (append) rows into this Kudu table.

We can also register our tables in Spark through Spark's read operation:

```
spark.read.options(kuduOptions).kudu.registerTempTable(kuduTableName)
```

By doing this, we can now insert directly into this table using Spark SQL syntax:

```
spark.sql(s"INSERT INTO TABLE $kuduTableName SELECT * FROM source_table")
```

The simplest way to read in the Kudu table and to obtain a DataFrame object to work with from our Kudu table is the following:

```
spark.read.options(kuduOptions).kudu
```

Finally, Kudu also supports predicate pushdown for predicates in the where clause, such as in the following statement:

```
val customerNameAgeDF = spark.
    sql(s"""SELECT name, age FROM $kuduTableName WHERE age >= 30""")
```

Spark uses data locality information from the Kudu master servers and will try to set work for specific data reads locally by Spark tasks that run on a given node. This improves overall read-in performance.

Impala with Kudu

Accessing Kudu through client APIs is certainly doable and recommended for your applications built on top of Kudu. Using frameworks such as Spark and Impala, on the other hand, not only allow you to process data in Kudu using a programmable, scalable framework like Spark, but can interact with Kudu using SQL syntax that takes advantage of the power of the massively parallel processing (MPP) capabilities of Apache Impala and SparkSQL.

Kudu integrates well with SQL frameworks due to its strongly typed fields and mostly rigid column structure that easily map to SQL engines. It has a concept of a table; however, this table is *not* the same table as an Impala table.

For example, Impala tables are defined on top of Kudu tables, meaning that the table name provided to Impala is not necessarily the table name of the Kudu table. For Impala, Kudu is another storage layer that it incorporates, similar to S3 or HDFS storage layers. Further, Impala has Serializer/Deserializer (SerDes) and record input formats that it can handle when the data is in S3 or HDFS. However, when it comes to Kudu, it interacts with Kudu as a separate storage layer that's capable of doing fast lookups but in particular, fast scans of large amounts of structured data. This allows for aggregate or analytic queries to be driven through Impala quickly and easily.

For example, an Impala table on top of Kudu might be defined as follows:

```
CREATE EXTERNAL TABLE `impala_kudu_table` STORED AS KUDU
TBLPROPERTIES(
    'kudu.table_name' = 'my_kudu_table',
    'kudu.master_addresses' = 'master1:7051,master2:7051,master3:7051');
```

From this definition, we can see that the Kudu table name is completely separate from the Impala table name. Next, we can also see that there's no need for us to define columns and data types for the columns, as those definitions are retrieved directly from the underlying Kudu table itself. Finally, the master addresses representing the Kudu cluster that are storing the Kudu table are specified. Hence, in a given Impala schema, you might have tables that actually exist in different Kudu clusters. That is not ideal, of course, because you lose data locality between the Impala daemons and the Kudu tablet servers. However, you have that kind of flexibility in this model.

Impala also provides predicate pushdown in queries you perform, where predicates are evaluated in the storage layer, Kudu, instead of having records flow back to Impala to *then* be applied. This can result in fantastic performance improvements.

You also can use Impala as a data movement utility, as you look to transfer data from one storage layer to the next. For example, having a table defined in HDFS can easily be used as the source table to read from while you insert the contents of your query into a Kudu table.

Joining datasets between Kudu, HDFS, and other storage engines is in fact encouraged, and execution plans will be built according to the storage layer being accessed for that portion of the query plan.

## CHAPTER 6

Table and Schema Design

In this chapter, we cover schema design in Kudu with the goal of explaining the basic concepts and primitives to make your project successful. An ideal schema would result in read and write operations spreading evenly across the cluster and also result in the minimum amount of data being processed during query evaluation. It's our belief that by understanding the basics described in this chapter, you will be closer to building an ideal schema and thus be on the pathway to success.

The Kudu project itself has fantastic schema design documentation (*https:// kudu.apache.org/docs/schema_design.html*), so even though there is some overlap, we will also focus on topics of particular importance and provide additional background.

In any data storage system, schema design is extremely important and the cause of many headaches and showstoppers. Poor schema design in relational databases can cause issues ranging from intensive resource consumption to data corruption. HBase and Cassandra require extensive knowledge of how the data will be accessed prior to designing a schema, and a deficiency here is the most common cause of project blockers due to slow query performance—almost always due to intensive resource consumption. In Kudu, schema design is as important, but Kudu provides some features these other systems don't provide to make a larger range of use cases possible.

Schema Design Basics

This section provides basics of Kudu schema design for readers who have not read the official schema design documentation:

- Tables require at least one primary key.
- Only primary keys are indexed (as of Kudu 1.6).
- You cannot update primary key.

- Only primary keys can be used for table partitioning either by hash or range.

- Most tables will be partitioned by hash, including time-series use cases that will also have a range partition. Note other use cases can use range partitioning.

- Each column has a type, encoding, and compression. Encoding has decent defaults and the default compression is none.

Table 6-1 show the possible encodings for each type.

Table 6-1. Column types

Column type	Encoding	Default
Boolean	Plain, Run Length	Run Length
8-bit signed integer	Plain, BitShuffle, Run Length	BitShuffle
16-bit signed integer	Plain, BitShuffle, Run Length	BitShuffle
32-bit signed integer	Plain, BitShuffle, Run Length	BitShuffle
64-bit signed integer	Plain, BitShuffle, Run Length	BitShuffle
UNIXTIME_MICROS (64-bit microseconds since the Unix epoch)	Plain, BitShuffle, Run Length	BitShuffle
Single-precision (32-bit) IEEE-754 floating-point number	Plain, BitShuffle	BitShuffle
Double-precision (64-bit) IEEE-754 floating-point number	Plain, BitShuffle	BitShuffle
UTF-8 encoded string (up to 64 KB uncompressed)	Plain, Prefix, Dictionary	Dictionary
Binary (up to 64 KB uncompressed)	Plain, Prefix, Dictionary	Dictionary

Schema for Hybrid Transactional/Analytical Processing

As discussed at length, Kudu is a column store that uses quorum-based replication to ensure data durability. It is used primarily for online analytical processing (OLAP) and Hybrid Transactional/Analytical Processing (HTAP)-style workloads. This section aims to discuss schema in an HTAP context. In short, the challenge for an HTAP system is to handle both operational work, with its small transitions, and updates and analytical work, with their large scans over a subset of columns.

First let's imagine an HTAP use case. A good one is an Internet of Things (IoT) device such as a connected car. In this use case, there are a few usage patterns:

- Engineers and data scientists want access to perform analytics across devices. Among other things, this allows the researchers to understand the impact of a defective part or to train a machine learning model.

- Customer support wants access to the *latest* data for a particular device so that they can troubleshoot the device for customers in real time.

- Management wants reports on aggregated data across devices.

- Customers want to access their data in the form of real-time dashboards and reports. Importantly, the customer could be shown slightly old data, but internet users are quickly being trained to expect all their data to be available in real time.

In the past, a highly complex system would be built to handle these use cases. We'd either build a Lambda architecture system or perform what is known as online transaction processing (OLTP)/OLAP split. Both these systems split the data into two different systems and because of this, there are many problems and complexities.

Lambda Architecture

Lambda architecture splits the data and workload into *speed* and *batch* layers. We use the speed layer for lookup queries and for analytics on the latest data, and we use the batch layer for analytics on the historical data. Two issues in particular arise from this:

- Many moving parts results in two code bases and extremely complex failure handling and operations. Few people, if any, like operating a Lambda architecture.
- As a longtime implementor of systems on immutable stores such as Hadoop Distributed Files System (HDFS) and Kafka, we can tell you that restatement is normal in use cases that are *never updated*.

OLTP/OLAP Split

In this system the latest data is stored in an OLTP relational database and then batch copied to an OLAP system for analytics *later*. Although this is the traditional method of performing analytics, it has many problems, some of which are described here:

- Analytical use cases don't get access to the latest data. This has real-world impact when an analytical question needs to be asked on the latest data, such as, "Did our software update cause this problem we are seeing?" Furthermore, management, like others, is becoming trained to expect data to be available in real time.
- Relational databases have a real scalability limit that often results in per-device data having a limited lifespan. This conflicts with users' expectations that they'll be able to see "their data" forever.
- IT must manage two systems and a complex data copy process.

Kudu allows us to address both of these use cases with a single system. By using a primary key that includes both the timestamp and device identifier we can efficiently query per-device data for customers and customer support. In addition, because Kudu was built for analytics, we can easily perform full scans on large subsets of the data for engineers, data scientists, and management.

This use case greatly benefits from using solid-state drives (SSDs) for storage because the per-device data will typically retrieve a large subset of the rows and result in a significant amount of disk seeks. However, longer term there is a design that could presumably reduce the benefit of SSD. As discussed earlier, fractured mirrors (*http://www.vldb.org/conf/2002/S12P03.pdf*) would result in one or two nodes in a quorum storing data as a row format, whereas the remainder would store data in a columnar format. OLAP-style workloads can target the columnar nodes, whereas OLTP workloads can target the row stores.

Primary Key and Column Design

The most important decision when deciding on your table's schema is your primary keys. You can use only primary keys as part of the partitioning scheme, but you cannot update them. Other columns can be updated via an UPDATE or UPSERT option. (We discuss partitioning later.) A Kudu table must have one or more columns defined as part of the primary key. Those columns are non-nullable, immutable, cannot be floating point or Boolean, and must define a unique row. However, perhaps even more important, because Kudu lacks secondary indexes (as of version 1.6), scans that lack predicates for all primary keys will be full table scans. For analytical queries this is acceptable, but it is not acceptable for queries you expect to perform like short lookups.

 In the following example, the word "continuous" is distinct from "batch."

Let's look at an example. We wrote the first revision of the Kudu lookup processor for StreamSets. StreamSets is a continuous ingest tool that allows you to perform record-wise transformations during the ingest process. A lookup processor allows developers to add additional fields to a record in a StreamSets data flow. Because StreamSets is a continuous ingestion process, performing a large amount of work on each record causes extremely long delays on ingest. As such, when developing the processor it's extremely important that the incoming record have values associated with each primary key so that the lookup completes by utilizing the primary key index and thus is fast enough to be performed on single records in a continuous manner. Given this, in StreamSets if an incoming record does not have all the required primary key values, it's sent to the error path.

Figure 6-1 shows the StreamSet lookup processor in action.

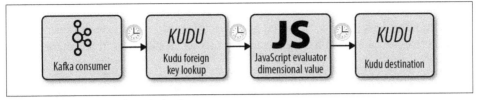

Figure 6-1. StreamSets Kudu lookup processor

Other Column Schema Considerations

For all columns, a big consideration is encoding and compression. These two trans-formations both reduce the size of data, but by different orders of magnitude and with different trade-offs. By this point in the book you are aware that Kudu is a col-umnar data store. Columnar data stores have a much wider array of encodings avail-able to them because values of the same type are stored in a sequence. Compression applies a generic algorithm to data to reduce the data size. Both mechanisms are used in columnar data stores, and some encodings include a compression algorithm.

In this section, we discuss a few encoding types in detail to help you understand how encoding differs from compression. We then discuss practice use cases for each encoding type. Kudu currently supports plain, run-length, BitShuffle, dictionary, and prefix encoding:

Plain encoding
> Data is encoded in its "natural" format. For example a 32-bit integer is encoded as a fixed-width 32 bits.

Run-length encoding
> Consecutive repeated values (runs) are stored as the value and the count. This type of encoding is effective when the column contains many repeated values when sorted by the primary key.

BitShuffle encoding
> BitShuffle combines a transformation with the generic compression algorithm LZ4. Values are rearranged to store the most significant bit of every value, fol-lowed by the second most significant bit, and so on. Afterwards, the result is LZ4 compressed. This type of encoding is effective when the column contains repeated values or values that change slightly when sorted by primary key.

Dictionary encoding
> Data is encoded by building a dictionary of unique values. Data is encoded by storing the index into the dictionary. This type of encoding is effective when a column contains a small number of unique values. If the column stores a unique value like a UUID, Kudu will fall back to plain.

Prefix encoding

Common prefixes are compressed in consecutive values. This type of encoding is effective for values that have a common prefix when stored by the primary key.

For each column, you need to either choose an encoding or take the default for the type. The default encodes are quite good; however, for strings you might consider changing the default. The default for string assumes strings of low cardinality. If you have unique strings with no common prefix—UUIDs, for example—you might consider plain encoding and LZ4 compression. If the strings have a common prefix, consider Prefix encoding and LZ4 compression. Note that if the column in question is the first column in the primary key, prefix encoding is likely the best bet because rows are sorted by primary key within tablets.

For example, we created three tables with a single string primary key and populated it with UUIDs using Python's `uuid.uuid4()` function, which doesn't have a common prefix. In the table, the first column was plain encoded LZ4 compressed, the second dictionary encoded LZ4 compressed, and the third prefix-encoded LZ4 compressed. The first two ended up being 102 MB, and the third 70 MB in size. The first two are the same because UUIDs are unique and thus dictionary encoding had no impact other than consuming CPU in its attempt at dictionary encoding. Because the table has a single column and rows are sorted by primary key within tablets, the prefix-encoded table performs the best.

As a second test, we then created the same three tables but added an integer, as the first column, to the primary key. The integer was plain encoded and uncompressed so it didn't vary across test tables. Plain encoding and dictionary encoding resulted in 180 MB of data, whereas prefix encoding resulted in 178 MB or about 1% better. To test CPU overhead of the encoding, we modified *src/kudu/cfile/encoding-test.cc* in Kudu to encode millions of random strings, and it appears there is about a 5% CPU encoding overhead for prefix encoding. It's difficult to say which would be more impactful to performance of a given use case, but given the trends of computer architecture, growing I/O bandwidth, and relatively limited growth in CPU performance, we would not prefix encode UUIDs unless it's the first column in a primary key or the UUID is a version with a common prefix.

In a moment, we help you visualize two encodings: run length and BitShuffle. Note, however, that these are not the implementation of these encodings Kudu uses, but vastly simplified versions for demonstration purposes only.

Let's discuss run-length encoding to understand how this differs from compression. First, let's assume that we have a list of 100 Boolean values. The first 50 are true, the following 49 are false, and the last value is true. If we use a 0 to represent false and 1 to represent true, we could encode the values in as one bit per value in binary as 111... 000...01, which consumes 100 bits of storage. Alternatively, we could run-length encode and store a value and a count. For example, let's assume that we store runs in eight bits (one byte). The first bit represents the truth value true or false, and the remaining seven bits are the number of true or false values. In seven bits, the maximum range we can store is 0 to 2^7 or 0 to 127. Using this encoding to store the previous sequence of Booleans, we'd store one byte to store the first run of trues, one byte to store the runs of falses, and then another byte to store the last true. In total, we'd consume 24 bits or 3 bytes. Compare that against the original 100 bits consumed by just storing true or false as one bit. Figure 6-2 shows a visual representation of run-length encoding.

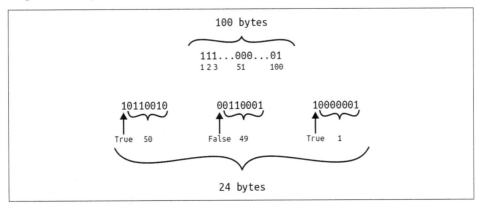

Figure 6-2. Run-length encoding

Now let's discuss BitShuffle. An interesting sidenote is that BitShuffle was published in 2015 and was developed with the goal of compressing data from the Canadian Hydrogen Intensity Mapping Experiment (*http://bit.ly/2KSEwEH*). It's great to see science benefiting the broader public. BitShuffle basically rearranges the bits in a given set of data so that it compresses better. The observation is that often numbers of a given column are highly correlated; for example, a monotonically increasing number. Given this, we can rearrange the bits so that the similar parts are together and the differences are at the end.

For example, suppose that we have three unsigned numbers of size: 1, 2, and 5 bytes. These in binary representation would be `00000001`, `00000010`, and `00000101`. This would be `000000010000001000000101` stored in a binary stream. Now let's transpose the bits to the most significant bit first, second most significant second, and so forth; we'd have `000000000000000001010101`. This would obviously compress much better, and indeed in this tiny example, BitShuffle increases the LZ4 compression by 50%. Of course, on read we need to reverse the transpose of the bits. Figure 6-3 shows a visual representation of BitShuffle encoding.

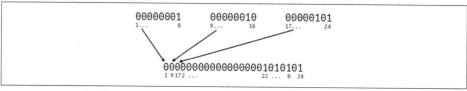

Figure 6-3. BitShuffle encoding

Which is better? As always, it depends. However, run length was commonly used for integers; thus many are likely wondering why Kudu's default for integers is BitShuffle, not run length. We believe the reason is that BitShuffle is a better general-purpose encoding. In the example that follows, we encoded two sets of numbers: one is a monotonically increasing set from 1 to 32,768, and the other is a set of positive random numbers less than 1,000,000. Both types are common in databases. For example, a primary key is often monotonically increasing integers, which real run-length encoding algorithms can handle efficiently. Relatively random positive numbers are common in foreign keys for dimension tables. As you can see, for our monotonically increasing data, run length outperforms BitShuffle by a factor of three times. However, they both perform quite well, compressing 32 K of data to less than 1 K. In the random small positive use case, the story is much different. BitShuffle gives us about 1.6 x compression, whereas run length actually increases the size of the data—we verified the increase in size is not due to LZ4. The source code for this exercise is in the book's code repository under *chapter6*, in the file *BitShuffleRunLengthComparison.java*. Table 6-2 summarizes the test's output.

```
==== Monotonically Increasing
Plain Size: 32768
Plain LZ4 Compressed Size: 32875
Plain Zlib Compressed Size: 16513
Plain Snappy Compressed Size: 32791
BitShuffled LZ4 Compressed Size: 993
RunLength Encoded LZ4 Compressed Size: 297
==== Random Small Positive
Plain Size: 32768
Plain LZ4 Compressed Size: 32898
Plain Zlib Compressed Size: 25887
Plain Snappy Compressed Size: 32794
BitShuffled LZ4 Compressed Size: 20662
RunLength Encoded LZ4 Compressed Size: 41172
```

Table 6-2. Summary of compression and encoding data

Data type	Encoding	Compression	Size	Percent of raw
Monotonically Increasing	Plain	None	32768	100%
Monotonically Increasing	Plain	LZ4	32875	100%
Monotonically Increasing	Plain	Zlib	16513	50%
Monotonically Increasing	Plain	Snappy	32791	100%
Monotonically Increasing	BitShuffle	LZ4	993	1%
Monotonically Increasing	Run Length	LZ4	297	3%
Random Small Positive	Plain	None	32768	100%
Random Small Positive	Plain	LZ4	32898	100%
Random Small Positive	Plain	Zlib	25887	79%
Random Small Positive	Plain	Snappy	32794	100%
Random Small Positive	BitShuffle	LZ4	20662	63%
Random Small Positive	Run Length	LZ4	41172	126%

Hopefully, you now see how encodings differ from compression. Compression can be applied to any kind of data in a generic fashion and depending on the dataset, it generally has less impact than encodings. In Kudu, except in the case of BitShuffle, which itself uses LZ4, compression is applied after the data has been encoded. Note that we do not recommend using another layer of compression on top of BitShuffle; however, at the time of this writing, Kudu will let you define a BitShuffle encoded column that is also compressed. Compression formats supported by Kudu are LZ4, Snappy, and zlib. Unless there are specific reasons, we stick with LZ4. It achieves similar compression to Snappy but is faster and thus consumes less CPU. Zlib consumes the most CPU, and you should avoid it. Generally speaking, BitShuffle is a good default encoding mechanism. Figure 6-4 shows Kudu allowing us to enable compression on top of BitShuffle.

Schema

Column	ID	Type	Encoding	Compression
col1	0	int64 NOT NULL	BIT_SHUFFLE	SNAPPY

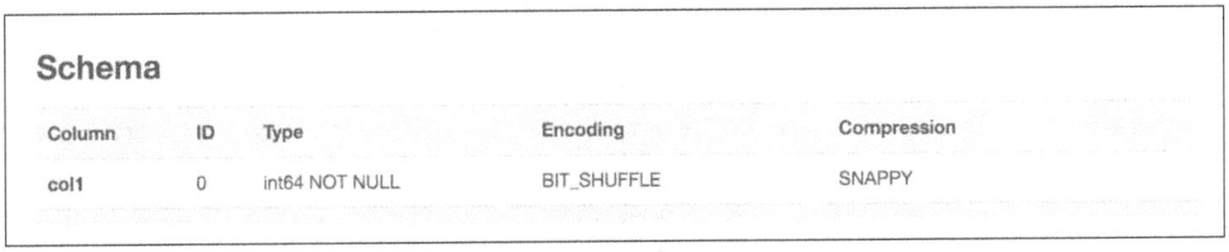

Figure 6-4. Kudu BitShuffle Snappy compressed column

Partitioning Basics

Data partitioning is the mechanism used to partition data into nonoverlapping independent sets. This is done for performance, data availability, and load balancing reasons. There are many such mechanisms; for example, round-robin partitioning separates data into *n* partitions by simply rotating which partition is to receive data on each assignment. For example, with three partitions (0, 1, 2) and five elements (a, b, c, e, f), data will be assigned as follows: (0 = a, e; 1 = b, f; 2 = c). The strong disadvantage of this partitioning scheme is that it's not possible to answer the question, "Which partition is *c* assigned to?" without consulting each and every partition. That is, it's not possible to "exclude" partitions from your search for *c*.

Range Partitioning

Range partitioning is fairly straightforward. For example, assume that we are trying to partition the integers 0 through 9 into two partitions. We could assign 0, inclusive, to 5, exclusive, as represented by the following interval notation [0,5) to partition 0. Furthermore, partition 2 could store [5,10). This schema works on noninteger data such as bytes, as well.

Hash Partitioning

Hash partitioning involves choosing a column to hash on and a number of buckets to distribute the data. Then, Kudu uses a hash function to decide in which bucket a given row should reside. Let's assume that we have a table with a single integer primary key that is hash partitioned and we've chosen four hash buckets (b0, b1, b2, b3). Now, let's assume that we have six rows with primary keys of (1, 12, 54, 99). Further let's assume that we have a function that, given an integer, simply returns the integer. In math, this is known as the *identity function*, which is a trivial hash function but a valid one.

Let's see how these rows distribute:

```
Key 1:  identity(1)  % 4 = 1 => Bucket b1
Key 12: identity(12) % 4 = 2 => Bucket b2
Key 54: identity(54) % 4 = 2 => Bucket b2
Key 99: identity(99) % 4 = 3 => Bucket b3
```

Kudu uses a hash function known as Murmur2, which is known as fast and high quality with few collisions.

Readers with HBase experience know about the issue of hotspotting, in which new primary keys are created toward the end of the key range. For example, in HBase, if your key is a timestamp and you store it as a string such as 20170910..., all new inserts will be sent to a single HBase Region that exists on a single server. To work around this, users must prefix or "salt" the keys with something like a hash bucket. The same thing could happen in Kudu, but Kudu makes the workaround for this issue vastly easier. You can combine partition schemes to work around this in Kudu. You simply need to add another key to your primary key and hash partition on that column. For example, in a time-series use case, you can define both the timestamp and some other column as primary keys and range partition on the timestamp and hash partition on the other column. No manual salting required!

Schema Alteration

Kudu supports fast schema alteration, meaning the alterations it supports won't cause the table to become locked for minutes or hours. This is because the data is not rewritten on modification, but later on compaction. Currently Kudu (as of version 1.6) supports the following modifications:

- Rename the table
- Rename primary key columns
- Rename, add, or drop nonprimary key columns
- Add and drop range partitions

If you'd like more detail about how schema changes are implemented, the design document (*https://github.com/cloudera/kudu/blob/master/docs/design-docs/schema-change.md*) is highly readable.

There are also a few things you should know when addressing Kudu from Impala. First know that Hive/Impala have the concept of *internal* and *external* tables. For internal tables Hive/Impala manage the storage, and for external tables they do not. This means that if you create a Hive/Impala internal table, it will expect to create the table for you; and when you drop the table in Hive/Impala, it will drop the corresponding Kudu table. You can move Hive/Impala Kudu tables to and from internal and external tables by modifying the table property EXTERNAL, which is a string Boolean (TRUE/FALSE). Changing the name of a Hive/Impala Kudu table, does not change the underlying Kudu table in case other clients are accessing it. You can change the underlying Kudu table name via the kudu.table_name table property. More details are available on the Kudu Impala integration (*https://kudu.apache.org/docs/kudu_impala_integration.html#_altering_table_properties*) page.

Best Practices and Tips

There are several best practices and tips/tricks to designing schemas in Kudu that we cover next. It's important to note that because Kudu is in its infancy, these best practices will change and grow as the community learns how to best utilize the technology in production.

Partitioning

Most tables will have at least one column that is hash partitioned and possibly another column that is range partitioned. It's rare for tables to have only range partitions. The reason is that the hash partition avoids hotspotting for many tables that are range partitioned. The canonical example of this is a time-series dataset for which new records are generated toward one end of the range.

Large Objects

Binary/string columns are limited to 64 KB uncompressed, meaning that the size check occurs before Kudu performs any compression. Although it's possible to increase this limit with an unsafe configuration flag, this limit is in place, today, because Kudu has not been tested with objects larger than 64 KB. As such, if you're storing larger binary/string objects, you can compress them *before* storing them in the data and then turn Kudu encoding to plain and leave column compression off. I've found that 64 KB of JSON, XML, or text significantly compresses with Gzip such that this limit is rarely hit. If the objects are much larger than 64 KB, store the object itself in HBase or HDFS and then store a foreign key.

decimal

decimal was added in version 1.7. It is a numeric data type with fixed scale and precision. You can use it in primary keys (whereas other types like float and double cannot) and it is available for use in C++, Java, Python, Impala, and Spark. This is a particularly useful data type for financial or other calculations for which the rounding behavior of float and double are impractical or even incorrect. Keep in mind that Kudu clients 1.6 or earlier cannot use tables in any way for tables that make use of decimals. Also, creating tables with decimals prevents the ability to downgrade to earlier releases of Kudu.

If you are using an earlier release prior to the introduction of decimal, float, and double are often used, but keep in mind they are not exact types and as such are not suitable for financial transactions. We store these values as a string and then cast them to decimal in Impala or SparkSQL. There is a performance hit because predicate evaluation for these columns will not be pushed down to Kudu, but it's working well for us at dozens of customers.

Unique Strings

If a table has a single string, primary key prefix encoding performs best. Otherwise, for this type, we use plain encoding and LZ4 compression.

Compression

BitShuffle columns are automatically LZ4 compressed. We turn on LZ4 compression for all other columns. LZ4 is generally faster than Snappy according to Percona's exhaustive tests (*http://bit.ly/2uguoLD*).

Object Names

Table names need to be unique across Kudu. If you create tables via Impala, Impala will prefix the table name with "impala::database.table." Because the database.table combination uniqueness is enforced by Impala, you won't run into trouble.

Make table and column names lowercase. This avoids confusion when users query a table in Impala (not case sensitive), but write to it via the API (case sensitive).

Number of Columns

Remember that in Kudu you should keep columns under 300. If you have source systems that have more than this, while pulling into Kudu, split the source system into buckets of 300 columns. Keep the primary key in each of them so that you can merge them back together with a view.

Binary Types

Keep in mind that Impala does not have a *binary* type. If you need to store a binary in a Kudu table, first ask yourself, "What am I going to use this for, and does it really need to be in Kudu?" If you end up needing it, create the table as a string type in Impala, base64 the binary array, and then insert. Be careful of the 64 K limit. In the near term, it might not make sense to have the binary in Kudu.

Network Packet Example

NetFlow is a data format that reflects the IP statistics of all network interfaces interacting with a network router or switch. NetFlow records can be generated and collected in near real time for the purposes of cybersecurity, network quality of service, and capacity planning. For network and cybersecurity analysts interested in this data, being able to have fast, up-to-the-second insights can mean faster threat detection and higher-quality network service.

The following example shows how combining hash or range partitioning can reduce the amount of data read for any query with a time-range predicate, thus improving read performance and also improving write performance by spreading writes across servers:

```
CREATE TABLE netflow (
id string,
packet_timestamp string,
srcaddr string,
dstas string,
dstaddr_s string,
dstport int32,
dstaddr string,
srcaddr_s string,
```

```
    tcp_flags string,
    dPkts string,
    tos string,
    engineid string,
    enginetype string,
    srcas string,
    packetid string,
    nexthop_s string,
    samplingmode string,
    dst_mask string,
    snmponput string,
    length string,
    flowseq string,
    samplingint string,
    readerId string,
    snmpinput string,
    src_mask string,
    version string,
    nexthop string,
    uptime string,
    dOctets string,
    sender string,
    proto string,
    srcport int32)
DISTRIBUTE BY HASH (id) INTO 4 buckets,
  RANGE (packet_timestamp)
  SPLIT ROWS ( ('2015-05-01'),
               ('2015-05-02'),
               ('2015-05-03'),
               ('2015-05-05')
             );
```

The table netflow is hash partitioned by the id field which is a unique key and should result in the rows being uniformly distributed among buckets and thus cluster nodes. Hash partitioning provides us high throughput for writes because (provided enough buckets) all nodes will contain a hash partition. Hash partitioning also provides for read parallelism when scanning across many ID values because all nodes that contain a hash partition will participate in the scan.

The table also has been range partitioned by time so that queries scanning only a specific time slice can exclude tablets not containing relevant data. This should increase cluster parallelism for large scans (across days) while limiting overhead for small scans (single day). Range partitioning also ensures partition growth is not unbounded and queries don't slow down as the volume of data stored in the table grows—because we would be querying only certain portions of data, and data is distributed across nodes by hash and range partitions.

The above table creation schema creates 16 tablets; first it creates four buckets hash partitioned by id field and then four range partitioned tablets for each hash bucket. When writing data to Kudu, a given insert will first be hash partitioned by the id field and then range partitioned by the `packet_timestamp` field. The result is that writes will spread out to four tablets (servers). Meanwhile read operations, if bounded to a single day, will query only the tablets containing data for the given day. This is important, because without much effort, we are able to scale out writes and also bound the amount of data read on time-series reads.

Although we didn't discuss it here, it's also interesting to remember that in addition to the analytical and ingest benefits of this partitioning scheme, similar to the IoT use case described earlier, we also can efficiently look up individual events, because the packet id is in the primary key.

Conclusion

As with all databases, schema design can make or break a high-performance use case. Kudu as a distributed database has some unique properties that need to take into account when you design. Furthermore, as a state-of-the-art database, there are new tuning options such as new column encodings and compression algorithms. After reading this chapter you should have a better understanding of the most important aspects of Kudu schema design.

## CHAPTER 7

Kudu Use Cases

Real-Time Internet of Things Analytics

You wake up in the morning, brush your teeth, grab some coffee, walk to the garage, get in the car, drive to work. Although this is your usual routine, today something feels off. You try to ignore it, but it keeps nagging you. It feels like you've forgotten something.

Your focus wanders from the radio DJ, to your plans for the weekend, to all the things you need to get done at work. But the nagging suspicion keeps coming back. What did I forget?

The nagging suspicion is interrupted by an alert on your phone. It's the garage door app on your smartphone! It's obvious now: you forgot to close the garage. It's your *Home Alone* moment. Even though you didn't forget your kid at home while on an overseas vacation, you did forget to close the garage door. Fortunately, it's the internet age and your garage door is connected to a smartphone app.

So, you pull over and, from your smartphone, you close your garage with the push of a button. All while 20 miles from home.

Just a few years ago, such situations meant driving all the way home, calling a neighbor, or spending the day with the nagging thought that someone is currently plundering your wife's new road bike and your son's golf clubs. But today, the crisis has been averted. You have data, analytics, and the Hadoop Ecosystem to thank.

Now, let's change gears and put ourselves in the shoes of the manufacturer of the garage door.

At your manufacturing plant in the Midwest, you've been building the world's best garage doors for decades. You can identify and hire the brightest minds in mechanical engineering to build actuators, motors, gears, and safety equipment—all things a world-class manufacturer needs. You had not anticipated that you'd be building data products, but here we are. Driven by changing consumer expectations and increased competition, data and analytics are mission-critical capabilities driving differentiation, efficiency, and sales.

Your data infrastructure must support the following:

A new consumer-facing smartphone app
  Prevents the aforementioned *Home Alone* moments.

Improved customer support
  The ability to remotely see the current state of a customer's device and the ability to remotely diagnose problems.

Improving quality
  Analysis across millions of garage doors deployed in the field. How are they used in practice? How can we identify problems with parts or usage?

Consumer marketing
  By understanding a specific customer's usage over time, how can we better market new, relevant products to them?

As a manufacturer, this is your first foray into building a data product, and you want a win. Having a simple, scalable, easy-to-maintain data infrastructure is paramount to the success of the project.

There are 100 million garage doors in the United States, and you own about 70% of the market. The garage doors are relaying information every 30 seconds. That's about 73 trillion rows per year. So, you have a scale problem and want to design this solution using cost-effective, scalable big data technology. The data includes a device identifier, report timestamp, status of the device, and various other information like fault codes and internal temperature, all of which you can see in Table 7-1.

Table 7-1. Column types

Device ID	Report time	Status	Fault code	Motor status	Travel mod	Heat sensor	$
583134	1492924860	0	0	11	0	22	$
583134	1492924890	0	0	11	0	22	$
583134	1492924920	1	0	11	0	23	$

Just a few years ago, you would have designed this system with two different storage layers. Rather than a Lambda architecture, Apache Kudu allows separate "speed" and analytical storage layers to be collapsed into a single datastore (Figure 7-1).

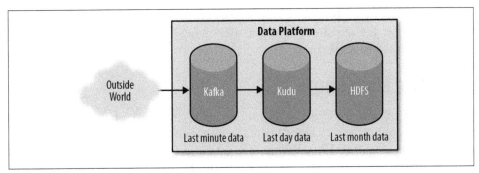

Figure 7-1. Diagram of Kudu-based Internet of Things architecture

As a prudent engineering-focused manufacturer, you know that one system will be easier than two. Kudu will make your data infrastructure faster to develop, easier and lower cost to maintain, and more adaptable for future use cases.

When designing our schema and partitioning strategy, we are going to consider the read and write workload, as discussed in Chapter 6. The workload of this application includes the following characteristics:

- High volume of reads and writes.
- All queries contain a time predicate; for example, show the most common fault code in the past three months, or scan all devices for the past 20 minutes to determine which garage doors have been left open.
- Many queries contain a short scan with a device identifier—customer service representatives and customers will commonly target the device identifier in their queries.

Because our workloads use the time and device as a predicate in most queries, our primary keys will be the report time and device ID. Because we have high throughput writes, our partitioning strategy includes a hash partition on the device identifier field. Assuming enough partitions, this ensures that our writes are spread among many tablet servers.

For our read workload, we want to avoid the overhead of short scans contacting too many tablet servers. For example, when customer service representatives or a user wants to know the current status of the device, a query might scan the last hour of data for a specific device ID, or about 120 rows. By range partitioning on the report time, rows with sequential timestamps are grouped together, resulting in performant, real-time lookups for specific users with short time ranges. Range partitioning also allows us to "age-off" older partitions and solves the issue of unbounded partitions.

Looking back on the goals of our data infrastructure, we have a single data repository that can support the broad needs of our user-facing customer service, quality, and consumer marketing applications.

Predictive Modeling

Let's go on a journey and pretend that we are going to start an online retailer from scratch. As an online retailer in today's market, we must provide relevant recommendations to our shoppers. We won't go into detail on how to build a recommender; many virtual and real trees have been felled in this endeavor. However, it's important to note that if you are building such a recommender today, you are very likely to be using the Hadoop platform to help do so, as shown in Table 7-2.

Table 7-2. Column types

User ID	Item ID	Score
123	342352342	0.23434343
123	123128933	0.3439292
124	957472924	0.62329292

The output of such a model is going to have three columns: User ID, Item ID, and Score. The User ID represents the user, the Item ID represents the item in the store, and Score represents some measure of likelihood of the given user liking the recommendation.

Then, after you have a score for every User ID and Item ID pair, you can begin making recommendations. That means being able to retrieve the highest scored items for a given user quickly. To give you some idea of scale, let's calculate the size of the dataset for Amazon.com. It has at present 480 million items and 304 million active users. This means that we'd have 145,920,000,000,000,000 or 145 quadrillion rows. If through columnar compression we reduced each row to 4 bytes per row, that would be 583 petabytes of data. Now this view is simplified; there are many techniques to reduce the size of this data, but it is true to say that recommender systems are classic *big data* systems.

Now that we understand the basics of the problem, how should we design it? First we begin with a batch system outside of the online retrieval side, which is always required. In this system, we need a batch storage layer to store transaction and page view logs and a batch execution layer to calculate the model. We use Hadoop Distributed File System (HDFS) or Amazon Web Services Simple Storage Service (Amazon S3) for storage and then Spark for batch execution. After we train the model, we need to publish it somewhere so that it can be accessed in real time. Traditionally, we'd write the model to HDFS/S3 and then export it to a relational database. This is a well-known approach, but it's complex to test and operate. Failing database export jobs are well-known happy-hour wreckers. This system is shown in Figure 7-2.

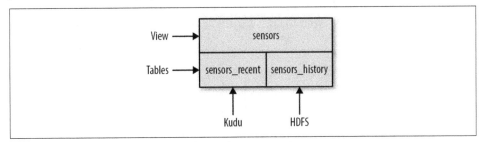

Figure 7-2. Diagram of recommender architecture 1.0

The first improvement to this model would be to eliminate the complex orchestration of exporting to another system. Because Kudu supports fast retrievals by primary key, we can eliminate the relational database and export to Kudu. This eliminates moving parts from our pipeline, which tends to lead to stability, as shown in Figure 7-3.

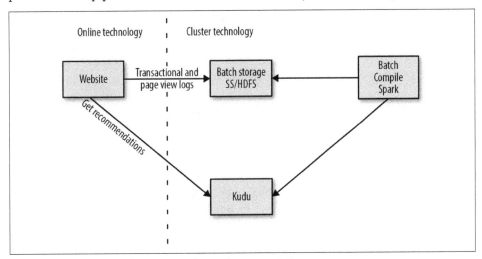

Figure 7-3. Diagram of recommender architecture 2.0

Although the first modification improved the data operations team's lives, the second improvement is going to focus on improving the business results and also management's view of how innovative our team is. At this point in time, we are still adding new data to the system only when we recalculate the scores, typically once each day or once per week. However, years ago, researchers became interested in possibly updating these batch-calculated results in a streaming or real-time context. As such, it's now possible to update the model in real time.

To implement this approach, we need a system for storing streaming data, as well. Kafka fits the bill. A happy side effect of this new architecture is that we can also store all transaction and page-view history in Kudu and provide this service to the website, as well. This eliminates the need for the website team to have its own historical store, as shown in Figure 7-4.

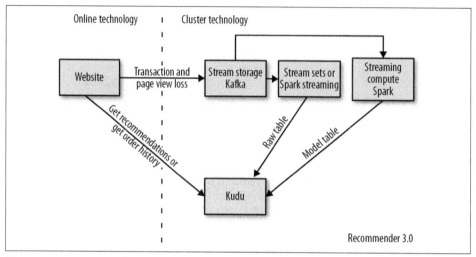

Figure 7-4. Diagram of recommender architecture 3.0

By using Kudu, we've been able to reduce complexity and improve our business by reducing data latency.

Mixed Platforms Solution

At this point of your reading, you probably understand the benefit of a Kudu-based design: fast, easy, open, structured, and so on. In this section, we give a high-level description of a use case in which we can use Kudu in conjunction with another storage engine.

One of the big benefits of Kudu is that because tables are structured and they have a primary key, data is always ordered. This is not the case for a storage system like Parquet files on HDFS. When data arrives fast and unordered, and analytics need to be performed on it, Kudu stays, by far, the most optimum platform! However, when data is already ordered, and retention policy makes the dataset grow to many terabytes, offloading Kudu into another format might be helpful.

This use case can be applicable for many different verticals; for example, when a large amount of data is coming from many different sensors or pieces of equipment and must be aggregated, ordered, and stored as fast as possible, to be available right away for analytics. You can imagine a utility company whose grid equipment is sending sensors information, but you can also imagine a telecommunications company whose antennas are sending data, or an oil company for which all the distribution points are sending real-time consumption information, and so forth. Different verticals, same concept.

Because data is coming for different sensors on different sites, it might arrive in the platform in an unsorted order. In a legacy design, we would store all of the data in a staging area, wait for all of the sites to have sent everything, and then sort the entire dataset before inserting it into tables and partitions. But because Kudu will store data ordered based on the key, there is no need to stage the data anywhere. We can insert all of the information into the system as soon as it arrives. Not only that, but we can retrieve it without any delay.

Even though the table and key design will be very similar to what we have seen in the previous sections, the difference here resides in the application design. Indeed, Kudu not being able to scale as far as what HDFS is capable of doing today, storing years of historical data requires offloading "old" Kudu data into another format. The idea behind the detailed design that we'll look at in a moment is to benefit from multiple tools' strengths. Here, we are going to use Kudu for its real-time incredibly fast analytic support, and HDFS for its almost endless scalability.

Figure 7-5 describes how data is flowing between the two platforms.

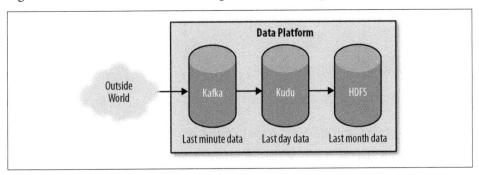

Figure 7-5. Multiplatform ingest

Most of the analytic requests are usually run against recent data. It is not common to run frequent requests against data that is many months or years old. Frequent requests are usually run against the last day's, last week's, last few weeks', or at maximum last month's data. Because Kudu is the fastest option for analytics, and because most of the requests are run over the last month's data, we are going to keep only the last month's data in Kudu. Past 31 days, once every 24 hours, the oldest day will be extracted from Kudu and exported to HDFS into an Impala Parquet table partition.

So, the next challenge will be related to the way we query the data. Because some is stored in Kudu and some is stored in HDFS, we need to find a way to provide a unified view to the query engine, where recent data will be retrieved on one side, and "cold" data on another side. We should be able to access both engines simultaneously to process data when a query covering both recent and old data is run.

Here, we will take advantage of the view feature of Impala.

Because our data is partitioned by date, and because the two platforms are storing very specific ranges of dates, all of the tables we will create will be partitioned by this criteria. In that way, we will create one table on top of the Kudu table, partitioned by date, and one table on top of the HDFS table, again, partitioned by date. Now, to be able to federate the two datasets, we just need to create a view on top of them! All requests to the dataset need to be performed only against that view. When only recent data is queried, only Kudu will be involved. However, when analytics are run for a longer period, the two platforms will participate, transparently, for the user.

Figure 7-6 shows how the tables are using the different storage platforms and how the view is federating them for the end user.

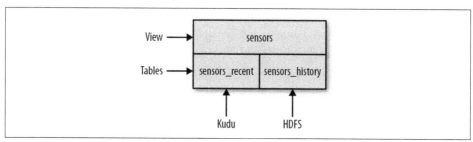

Figure 7-6. Multiplatform tables and view

Such a design has multiple benefits:

- It allows very fast and efficient access to the recent (and mostly used) data.
- The implementation is very simple. It requires only an ingestion pipeline—from Kafka to Kudu—and an offload Extract, Transform, and Load (ETL)—from Kudu to HDFS. We can do the offload ETL using a very simple SQL request.
- It allows a very flexible scalability. Indeed, when Kudu scalability is increased, more data can be kept in the Kudu cluster. When the retention policy changes, it's very simple to adjust that on the HDFS side.

Index

About the Authors

Jean-Marc Spaggiari, an early adopter of Kudu, works as a principal solutions architect for Cloudera to support Hadoop, Kudu, HBase, and other tools through technical support and consulting work. His deep knowledge of HBase and HDFS allows him to better understand Kudu and its applications.

Jean-Marc's primary role is to support HBase users over their HBase cluster deployments, upgrades, configuration, and optimization, as well as to support them regarding HBase-related application development. He is also a very active HBase community member, testing every release from performance and stability standpoints. However, with Kudu being geared to quickly penetrate the market, he will also begin recommending, building demo applications, and deploying proof of concepts around it.

Prior to Cloudera, Jean-Marc worked as a project manager and as a solutions architect for CGI and insurance companies. He has almost 20 years of Java development experience. In addition to regularly attending Strata+Hadoop World and HBaseCon, he has spoken at various Hadoop User Group meetings and many conferences in North America, usually focusing on HBase-related presentations and demonstrations. Jean-Marc is also the author of *Architecting HBase Applications* (*http://bit.ly/archi tect_hbase_apps*) (O'Reilly, 2016).

Mladen Kovacevic comes from a development background in RDBMS technology and sees Kudu as a game changer in the Hadoop ecosystem. He has presented Kudu at several local meetups, presented on the state of Spark on Kudu during its beta while providing feedback early enough to ensure Spark with Kudu is a first-class citizen at its launch. He is a contributor to Apache Kudu and Kite SDK projects and works as a solutions architect at Cloudera. Mladen's experience includes years of RDBMS engine development, systems optimization, performance, and architecture, including optimizing Hadoop on the Power 8 platform while developing IBM's Big SQL technology.

Brock Noland followed Kudu months before the first line of code was written, by following Todd Lipcon's paper reading habits. Brock is chief architect of phData, a pure-play Hadoop Managed Service Provider. Prior to founding phData, Brock spent four years at Cloudera as a trainer, solution architect, engineer, sales engineer, and engineering manager. Brock is a cofounder of Apache Sentry and Apache Project Committee Member on Apache Hive, Parquet, Crunch, Flume, and Incubator. Brock was a mentor to Kudu in the incubator and currently mentors Apache Impala (incubating). In addition, he is a member of the Apache Software Foundation.

Brock is a frequent public speaker, having appeared at dozens of conferences including HBaseCon, numerous Hadoop User Groups, and other conferences.

Ryan Bosshart is the CEO of phData and a former principal systems engineer at Cloudera. Ryan has spent the last 10 years building and designing distributed systems. At Cloudera, Ryan led the field storage specialization team where he focused on Apache HDFS, HBase, and Kudu. He has worked with many early users of Kudu to build their relational, time-series, IoT, or real-time architectures. He has seen first-hand Kudu's ability to improve performance and simplify architectures. Ryan is a co-chair of the Twin Cities Spark and Hadoop User Group and the author of the training video "Getting Started with Kudu" (*http://bit.ly/getting-started-kudu-video*) (O'Reilly).

Colophon

The animal on the cover of *Getting Started with Kudu* is the greater kudu (*Tragelaphus strepsiceros*). One of the largest species of antelope, the greater kudu is found in woodlands, hills, and mountains across eastern and southern Africa.

The frame of the greater kudu is narrow and long-legged. Its coloring is dark gray or brown with white vertical stripes running along its sides and a white chevron extending between the eyes. The bull has thicker fur than the cow, including a short mane that grows along the front of its neck, and has spiraling horns that extend upward to a single point after coiling two and a half times.

While the males are solitary, female kudus typically travel in groups of 6 to 10, though larger groups have been reported. Mating occurs at the end of the rainy season, and calving occurs eight months later. Mothers hide their young in tall grass and other foliage during their first month of life, but calves mature quickly and are independent at the age of six months.

In the past decade, the global population of greater kudu has thinned slightly due to hunting, disease, and habitat loss, though some areas previously too dry for kudus to inhabit are now viable thanks to wells and irrigation systems. The unique horns of the kudu are prized by poachers and are frequently used to create Shofars (Jewish ritual horns that are blown during Rosh Hashanah).

Many of the animals on O'Reilly covers are endangered; all of them are important to the world. To learn more about how you can help, go to *animals.oreilly.com*.

The cover image is from *Meyers Kleines Lexicon*. The cover fonts are URW Typewriter and Guardian Sans. The text font is Adobe Minion Pro; the heading font is Adobe Myriad Condensed; and the code font is Dalton Maag's Ubuntu Mono.

Learn from experts.
Find the answers you need.

Sign up for a **10-day free trial** to get **unlimited access** to all of the content on Safari, including Learning Paths, interactive tutorials, and curated playlists that draw from thousands of ebooks and training videos on a wide range of topics, including data, design, DevOps, management, business—and much more.

Start your free trial at:

oreilly.com/safari

(No credit card required)

CPSIA information can be obtained
at www.ICGtesting.com
Printed in the USA
BVHW05s0635130718
521524BV00010B/33/P

9 781491 980255